what your soul needs for stressful times

OTHER WORKS BY HOLLEY GERTH

You're Already Amazing

You're Made for a God-Sized Dream

You're Going to Be Okay

What Your Heart Needs for the Hard Days

You're Loved No Matter What

Fiercehearted

Hope Your Heart Needs

Strong, Brave, Loved

The Powerful Purpose of Introverts

what your soul needs for stressful times

60 POWERFUL TRUTHS
to Protect Your Peace

HOLLEY GERTH

Revell

a division of Baker Publishing Group
Grand Rapids, Michigan

248.4

© 2021 by Holley, Inc.

Published by Revell
a division of Baker Publishing Group
PO Box 6287, Grand Rapids, MI 49516-6287
www.revellbooks.com

Printed in the United States of America

Library of Congress Cataloging-in-Publication Data
Names: Gerth, Holley, author.
Title: What your soul needs for stressful times : 60 powerful truths to protect your peace / Holley Gerth.
Description: Grand Rapids, Michigan : Revell, a division of Baker Publishing Group, [2021] | Includes bibliographical references.
Identifiers: LCCN 2021003814 | ISBN 9780800738532 (cloth) | ISBN 9781493431915 (ebook)
Subjects: LCSH: Peace of mind—Religious aspects—Christianity—Meditations. | Conflict management—Religious aspects—Christianity—Meditations.
Classification: LCC BV4908.5 .G49 2021 | DDC 248.4—dc23
LC record available at https://lccn.loc.gov/2021003814

21 22 23 24 25 26 27   7 6 5 4 3 2 1

contents

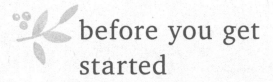# before you get started

For additional tools and resources that go with this book, visit holleygerth.com/stress.

introduction

What's causing you stress right now? Maybe it's a bad day or a busy schedule, the headlines on your television or the news you got from your doctor, family challenges or the latest project at work. You find yourself asking questions like . . .

What's going to happen?

How will this all work out?

Why do I feel so tired sometimes?

If that sounds like you, then this little book is an invitation to pause for a few moments of peace and strength each day. As a bestselling author, counselor, and life coach, I've worked with thousands of people who feel like you do. I've personally struggled to deal with stress in my life too. You're not the only one, and you don't have to handle this alone.

I've learned how you can deal with the stress in your life, and I'm excited to share it with you! I'll give you spiritual truth to soothe your soul and practical tools to apply that will make a difference. You really can live with more peace and less pressure, more calm and less chaos, more worship and less worry.

Imagine waking up to each new day with more hope and facing the future with confidence, even when life is hard or the world seems to be falling apart. Imagine being able to give your friends and family the steady support they need in *their* stressful times.

Stress is inevitable, but letting it control our lives is optional. You've already taken the first step toward a new way of living by reading these words. I'll give you what you need to keep moving forward no matter what happens.

Let's start this journey together today.

1

what you need in every stressful moment

God replied to Moses, "I AM WHO I AM. Say this to the people of Israel: I AM has sent me to you."

Exodus 3:14

Think of the last moment when you experienced stress. It could have been at home or in traffic, in your kitchen or in a conference room, in the hallway of a hospital or as you scrolled through social media. It might even be right now as you're reading these words.

What do all the times we experience stress have in common? The outcome feels uncertain. We don't know if our dream will succeed or fail, if the conflict in our relationship will get resolved, or if the test result will come back the way we'd hoped.

Humans feel stress when we experience uncertainty, and there's plenty of it in our world right now. It seems in the middle of all the challenges we face, some people have unshakable faith, that they never struggle with questions or doubts, fears or messy spiritual failures. It's best you know right up front that I'm not one of them.

Instead, I often find myself worrying about the future. I picture the worst-case scenario—the world falls apart, completely runs out of coffee, or I make an epic and unredeemable mistake. Then I start asking, "Where are you, God? Why won't you help me?"

In those moments, it helps to remember that when Moses asked God his name, the answer was simply, "I AM." Why does this matter in stressful moments? Because I AM is *present tense*.

God's name is not I Was.

His name is not I Will Be.

His name is I AM.

This means the only place we can fully experience the presence of God is the present. So, of course, it feels like he's not in our imaginary, worst-case scenario future. When we get to tomorrow, he will be there. But today he is exactly where we need him to be—with us.

As Melissa Spoelstra, author of *The Names of God* study, says, "When Moses needed confirmation, Yahweh said, 'Whatever you need, I AM.' If you need a provider, I AM. If you need help, I AM. If you need deliverance, I AM."[1] Moses wasn't in church or at a spa getting a pedicure when God spoke the name "I AM" to him. He was in a desert—a dry, lonely, difficult place. So we can take comfort in knowing God is with us even in our hard places. Our challenges do not change his character or commitment.

Paul writes in Romans 8:38, "I am convinced that nothing can ever separate us from God's love. Neither death nor life, neither angels nor demons, neither our fears for today nor our worries about tomorrow—not even the powers of hell can separate us from God's love."

Here's what we all need to know in every stressful moment:

God is with me right now.

God is with *you* right now.

And whatever tomorrow brings, he will be there too.

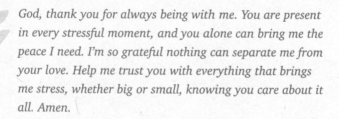

God, thank you for always being with me. You are present in every stressful moment, and you alone can bring me the peace I need. I'm so grateful nothing can separate me from your love. Help me trust you with everything that brings me stress, whether big or small, knowing you care about it all. Amen.

What's one thing you hope to gain from going through this book?

_____

_____

_____

HE'S WITH US IN THE BIG AND THE SMALL, leaving His fingerprints on every page of the story, forever reminding us: Remember My goodness here. Look around. Do you see Me? I'll hang the clouds in the sky and fling stars into the velvet night all so that you remember in both daylight and darkness, I'm with you always.

KAITLYN BOUCHILLON

2

less stress, more peace

Peace be with you, dear brothers and sisters.

Ephesians 6:23

What *is* stress? We describe everything from awkward conversations to major catastrophes as "stressful." That's actually appropriate, because experts define stress as the response our minds and bodies have to pressure. When we experience worry, fear, or anxiety, that's the psychological side of stress. When our hearts pound, hands shake, and thoughts race, we're being impacted by the physical part of stress.

While *stress* has been present throughout human history, that specific term has been used for less than one hundred years. Hans Selye, a Hungarian doctor, first came up with it in 1936 to describe a set of symptoms he repeatedly noticed in patients even though they had different illnesses. Because of stress's medical origin, we tend to think of it in negative terms—like a sickness we need to cure. And many of the most common causes of stress *are* negative, including personal problems, professional losses, and unexpected events like pandemics.

But stress itself is neutral. We also experience stress in positive situations like getting married, having a baby, being promoted at work, and moving to a new place. Stress is part of every worthwhile endeavor, from making a new friend to winning an Olympic gold medal.

In other words, stress actually has a purpose. It points out what matters most to us. It helps us identify possible threats. It prepares us for action. *Our natural human stress response is God-given.* He hardwired it into our brains and bodies. We need it to survive.

But we're fallen, broken people in a fallen, broken world, and sometimes a response that's intended to be helpful becomes a hassle and a headache (literally). Thankfully, God also gives us what we need to manage our stress, to make it work for us rather than against us.

Understanding stress matters, because stressed-out people often experience guilt or shame about the way they feel. Or they become determined to get rid of stress completely. But what we really need is to know how to make stress work for us, to keep it from wearing us out and bossing us around. That *is* possible, but it takes spiritual truth, psychological insights, and practical tools—all of which are coming in the pages ahead.

Think of your natural stress response like a wild horse. It can trample your yard and throw you onto the dirt. But it can also be tamed. And when that happens, it has surprising potential to help you move forward in life. What makes the difference? *Who's in control*. God will help you show your stress who's boss.

God, you know every detail of my life. You know the pressures I have, the challenges I face, and the moments when I grow tired and weary. You don't condemn me for experiencing stress; instead, you come alongside me to lead me back toward peace. Guide me on this journey. I give all that concerns me to you. Amen.

What have you been taught about stress? What's one new thing you learned about it today?

_____

_____

_____

HOW YOU THINK ABOUT STRESS AFFECTS everything from your cardiovascular health to your ability to find meaning in life. The best way to manage stress isn't to reduce or avoid it, but rather to rethink and even embrace it.

KELLY MCGONIGAL

3

helpful responses you can use

Let God transform you into a new person by changing the way you think.

Romans 12:2

I'm writing my ebook *Fear, I'm Over You* from my upstairs office on a sunny day. Outside everything looks the same. The Canadian geese that come to our pond every year have built their nest in the usual spot. The dogwood tree on the corner is in bloom. The turtles are lined up in the sun like teenagers at the beach. But, really, nothing is the same. Because I'm writing in the beginning stages of the COVID-19 pandemic. School is out. Restaurants are closed. Social distancing is suddenly the norm.

When I ventured to the grocery store for a few necessities, I could feel the fear like electricity in the air. When I looked at social media later that day, I could sense it too. In times like this, how do our brains respond?

Most of us are familiar with the fight-or-flight response. It's necessary for our survival. If a bear came charging out of the woods at us, we would react instantly by fleeing or becoming aggressive. I see versions of this response now, as some people buy all the toilet paper even though someone else might need it (fight) while others ignore what's going on (a form of flight).

But is fight-or-flight our only option? Thankfully, no, our brains have two other responses to stress that can prove much more helpful.

The first is the challenge response. Think of a time when you were afraid but also determined to take action. Examples would include an athlete before a big game, a presenter preparing to give a speech, or a parent handling a crisis involving their child. The difference in the challenge response is that we tell ourselves, "I've got this" or, as believers, "I've got this because God's got me."

Health psychologist and author Kelly McGonigal says,

> Like a fight-or-flight response, a challenge response gives you energy and helps you perform under pressure. Your heart rate still rises, your adrenaline spikes, your muscles and brain get more fuel, and the feel-good chemicals surge. But it differs from a fight-or-flight response in a few important ways: You feel focused but not fearful. You also release a different ratio of stress hormones, including higher levels of DHEA, which helps you recover and learn from stress. This raises the growth index of your stress response, the beneficial ratio of stress hormones that can determine, in part, whether a stressful experience is strengthening or harmful.[1]

Making a plan or asking ourselves, "What's one helpful action I can take right now?" helps our brains move into the challenge response.

The second alternative response our brains have to stress is called tend-and-befriend. We see this during any disaster when the helpers appear. When we assist others, our brains release oxytocin, which is sometimes called the cuddle hormone. It bonds us to others, and it's good for us personally; it can literally strengthen our hearts. Asking, "Who can I help right now?" helps shift our brains out of fight-or-flight mode. McGonigal says, "When you help someone else in the middle of your own distress, you counter the downward spiral of defeat."[2]

We all experience the fight-or-flight response, especially when the unexpected happens, but we don't have to stay in it. God said he'll take care of the birds and flowers I see outside my window. That, too, is still the same. He also takes care of us in many ways—including giving us remarkable, adaptable brains.

God, thank you for giving me a brain that can respond and adapt in many ways to whatever happens. When I feel stuck in fear, help me see it as a challenge that you and I can handle together so I can take action. And give me the courage to help others, because we are better and braver together. Amen.

What's a time when you chose the challenge response?
What's a time when you chose the tend-and-befriend
response?

_____

_____

_____

MANY OF THE THINGS THAT HAPPEN TO US are beyond
our control. . . . What matters is how we respond.

CAROLINE TESELLE

4

what true peace means

The LORD gives his people strength.
The LORD blesses them with peace.

Psalm 29:11

I recall a holiday season when Mark and I braved a local shopping area for some last-minute gifts. We braced ourselves for big crowds, long lines, loud songs playing over store speakers, and irritable drivers fighting to get the last parking spot. When we walked through our door an hour later, I took a deep breath and thought, *Peace at last.*

In our culture, we tend to think of peace as the absence of what troubles us. The blaring music gets turned off. The crowd thins out. The pace of our life slows down. But when Mark and I went to church that night, our wise pastor, Mark Schatzman, talked about what God really means when he says he will give us peace.

The biblical word for peace is *Shalom*, and while it's difficult to translate into our language, it essentially means wholeness and well-being. Theologian Tim Keller says, "Shalom experienced is multidimensional, complete well-being—physical, psychological, social, and spiritual; it flows from all of one's relationships being put right—with God, within oneself, and with others."[1]

What strikes me most when I read this is how often I settle for less than Shalom. I'm content with a shallow, surface-level peace. If I'm gut-honest, I even feel a bit nervous about the idea of Shalom. I'm a woman who knows how to work hard and fight harder. I'm used to my faith feeling like a battleground. If life is calm and things are good, I start wondering what will go wrong.

I tend to focus on the part of the gospel that is the cross. Yet sometimes in doing so, I forget that part of the purpose of the cross is to bring us Shalom.

> The punishment that brought us peace was on him,
> and by his wounds we are healed. (Isa. 53:5 NIV)

The story of Scripture starts with Adam and Eve in the garden, a place of complete peace. It ends in heaven, also a place of well-being and wholeness. It seems God is intent on seeing his people thrive, whatever it takes.

This doesn't mean we'll experience Shalom fully in this world. But there's something comforting in knowing that God is always working to bring us closer to it until we're Home forever.

> Great is the LORD,
>> who delights in blessing his servant with peace!
>> (Ps. 35:27)

We will go *through* hardship and suffering in this life. But peace is the place God has for us to dwell.

If we're in a season where life is happy, then that means we embrace it without fear or apology. We receive the gifts God is bestowing on us. We celebrate and savor every moment. We let the joy we feel now be a small preview of what we'll one day experience forever.

If we're in a season where life is hard and stressful, then that means we let Shalom be our hope. As Mark Schatzman said, "God makes peace out of our pieces."[2] No matter how broken we feel now, we can trust one day we'll be whole and that all will be well.

Yes, I thought for so long that peace was the absence of something. I know now that it's the presence of Someone. A God who loves us. A God who is for us. A God who is making all things new, including me and you.

God, you don't just give me peace; you are my peace.
Thank you that what you offer is so much deeper and
greater than I often know. I ask that you give me Shalom
so that no matter what my circumstances might be, I can
know that all will be well and I will be whole. Amen.

How have you defined peace? How would you do so now, based on what you just read about the meaning of Shalom?

_____

_____

_____

SHALOM IS GOD AND SHALOM COMES FROM GOD. We will never find rest or peace or wholeness in any other person, thing, or circumstance. It has always come from Him. He gives us peace and He sustains our peace. The world could be raging around us, but if our gaze is fixed on Him, we will not be moved.

KARINA ALLEN

5

the power of your perspective

For as he thinks in his heart, so is he.

Proverbs 23:7 NKJV

Years ago, my in-laws bought a beautiful SUV with pristine paint and not a dent in sight. They came to visit us for the weekend, and my mother-in-law needed to run an errand. She offered to let me drive. I promptly backed the aforementioned SUV directly into a trailer parked behind it. I cried. My mother-in-law might have too. In the moment after the incident, I told myself things like "You're such a mess! You always do stuff like this. You're never going to get it together."

Years later, my in-laws were in town again and we were heading out for a day at the lake. I had a sudden craving for a latte, so we pulled into the parking lot for a local coffee shop. I made my purchase and exited, only to discover my family talking to a stranger. Someone pointed to the bumper of our SUV, and I could see the crumpled metal and shattered headlight. The responsible party said, "I didn't see you in the rearview mirror. It's a work truck I've never driven before, and I'm not used to it. I wish I had backed out slower."

I stood there, coffee in hand, and considered our very different explanations of two strikingly similar events. Back in graduate school, I learned about research by a psychologist named Martin Seligman. He asserted that there are two distinct ways of explaining events in our lives. With the first style, pessimism, people see unfortunate events as personal, permanent, and pervasive. In other words, those with this style believe it's their fault, it will last forever, and it affects every area of their lives (see my response to backing into that trailer as an example).[1]

With the second style, optimism, people see those same events as external, temporary, and specific. In other words, they attribute the cause to something outside themselves, and they believe whatever happened won't last forever and that whatever happened is only related to this individual situation (see the response of the man who backed into Mark's SUV as an example).

This optimism is not the stereotypical kind where someone ignores reality and insists everything is good all the time. None of us want to be that way, so put that definition of optimism out of your mind. What we're talking about actually gives us a *more* realistic view.

Seligman found that those with the pessimistic style were more prone to anxiety, depression, and even physical illness.[2] They were more likely to quit jobs, not push through obstacles, and give up.[3] Here's the good news: we can change our style. Doing so begins with recognizing our natural stress response. If we tend to react with a pessimistic style, then we can pause and choose to process events in a different way. We can ask the following questions:

- *What external factors contributed to this?* (Example: I was driving an unfamiliar car, and the trailer was parked in my blind spot.)
- *Will this really last forever?* (This is unfortunate, but it can be fixed in a few days.)
- *Does this really affect every area of my life?* (One bad moment as a driver doesn't make me a bad person.)

The goal of this reflection is not to say, "I'm fine!" with a fake smile on our face. It's also not about getting out of our responsibilities or passing the blame. Both the man in the parking lot and I ended up paying for new bumpers.

Explaining events differently simply helps us be more resilient and minimizes the long-term damage to our emotional, mental, and physical health as well as to our relationships. It decreases our anxiety and helps us fight off depression. Also, while Seligman calls this optimism, it sure feels a lot to me like living in grace. As believers, we aren't limited to just "pessimist" or "optimist." We can go above and beyond either because we're indwelled by and empowered through the Spirit.

Sometimes I'm still tempted to look at what happens in my life as personal, permanent, and pervasive. We all have this tendency. When our spouse leaves. When our evaluation report at work is not what we had hoped. When our teenager yells and then slams the door. When we get laid off. When our friend stops returning our calls. When we spill the milk.

We often can't control what happens to us. But we can control what we think about it. And that can make all the difference.

God, you have given me a powerful mind that shapes how I view myself and my circumstances. When I start to give in to negativity and self-criticism, shift me back toward grace and compassion. I so often do this for others, but it's much harder to do for myself. Empower me to do so. Amen.

Think of a recent mistake you made or an unfortunate circumstance you experienced. How did you explain it to yourself? If you leaned toward the pessimistic style, write a new explanation below that's more optimistic (you can use the three questions from the devotion to help).

_____

_____

_____

IT'S THE CYNICS WHO HAVE A LIMITED, bruised vocabulary of *no*. It can seem easier to reject the world before the world hurts you again. It's the brave who say a prayerful *yes*, the brave and wise who believe that the faith-filled *yes* is what heals things. It's the brave and free who are the optimists.

ANN VOSKAMP

6

satisfy your soul thirst

He lets me rest in green meadows;
he leads me beside peaceful streams.

Psalm 23:2

I'm not an athletic sort of person. But I am married to one. And in an attempt to bond with my husband, I agreed to do a charity bike ride. I grew up in Texas, where the roads are smooth and the ground is flat. I'm still adjusting to the idea that this is not the case in other places, such as the one where we live. This ride had several distances to choose from, and Mark picked the longest—one hundred miles. This felt to me like a form of cruel and unusual punishment for one's behind. So I chose the shortest distance—twenty miles—which still felt monumental to me.

I arrived at the starting line just as the sun started to lighten the sky. I had risen as well, but I was certainly not shining. We began pedaling, and I noticed water stations along the route. I watched the speedier bikers roar up to them, grab a paper cup held out by a volunteer, toss the contents back in one great gulp, and carry on their way. It made me giggle a bit, because most of the water ended up on the rider's face and clothes and the ground. But slowing down for more just wasn't an option. (Sidenote: these stations also had tiny cups full of pickle juice. Apparently, the high salt content in it can make muscle cramps go away. Blech. I'm not that hardcore.)

Something about the riders zipping through the water stations felt familiar. Only later did I realize that I've lived through seasons when I've done the same—when everything has been rush-rush, hurry-hurry, stress-stress until my soul has felt parched. Perhaps that's why this picture the psalmist shares is so reassuring to me:

> He lets me rest in green meadows;
>> he leads me beside peaceful streams. (Ps. 23:2)

The metaphor here is about a shepherd and sheep. A modern-day sheep rancher says, "Sheep prefer to drink still water as opposed to water from a moving stream."[1] It seems it's easier for humans and sheep to receive what they need when there's not a rush.

We may think we have to settle for a quick sip, that God's priority is for us to cover as much ground as we can in as little time as we can. But his true invitation is for us to slow down, drink deep, and take all the time we need. Three times throughout Scripture God gives us this offer.

> Is anyone thirsty?
>> Come and drink. (Isa. 55:1)

> Jesus stood and shouted to the crowds, "Anyone who is thirsty may come to me!" (John 7:37)

> Let anyone who is thirsty come. Let anyone who desires drink freely from the water of life. (Rev. 22:17)

This is the miracle and mystery: God is pointing us not to an external source but to *himself*. He is "the LORD, the fountain of living water" (Jer. 17:13), and "when he said 'living water,' he was speaking of the Spirit" (John 7:39). He's not the volunteer standing by the side of the road with a cup in hand. He is the water itself, the One we thirst for with all our being.

Mark and I both finished our rides. We felt happy and satisfied. Pushing through and going fast is a fun way to spend a Saturday. But, I'm learning, it's a hard way to spend a life.

Pastor and author John Ortberg once asked theologian Dallas Willard what he needed to do to be spiritually healthy. Willard replied, "You must ruthlessly eliminate hurry from your life."[2] That's not the message we get from the world around us. We hear, "Go faster, do more, get to the finish line." What a relief to know we serve a God who instead simply says, "Anytime you're thirsty, anytime you need to receive, slow down and come to me."

God, you know how easy it is for humans to get caught up in moving fast and going far. In every moment, whether I'm busy or being still, help me remember that when my heart is weary and my soul is thirsty, I can come to you. You offer me what I most need to receive, what I can't get anywhere else. Amen.

Pause and take a deep breath. Let yourself sit in silence and stillness with Jesus for a moment before you move on with your day. What is your soul thirsty for right now?

_____

_____

_____

WE ALL HAVE TIMES when we are spiritually thirsty, when daily struggles and distractions can keep us from Him. We may not even realize how dehydrated we've become. We seem fine. We look fine. We think we are filling ourselves up, yet the insatiable thirst continues. We become parched and weak because there is no substitute for the refreshment only God can provide. Christ has come to give us living water and to give it to us in abundance.

JENNIFER UECKERT

7

understanding anxiety

A peaceful heart leads to a healthy body.

Proverbs 14:30

In third grade, I had a series of inexplicable stomachaches. I recall frequently asking my teacher if I could go to the nurse's office and walking down a hallway by the cafeteria that smelled like floor cleaner and instant mashed potatoes. Fortunately, I had a kind school nurse, one who took pity on me and let me lie down on a little mattress in a quiet room. My parents became concerned and took me for a series of tests. But no cause could ever be found, and the doctor finally shrugged and said, "Stress."

I happened to mention this at a writers' retreat a few years ago, and one after another of my creative, introverted friends said, "Me too." The symptoms varied—some had headaches, others back pain—but around the age of eight, all of us began to experience physical symptoms of anxiety. Creative introverts tend to have sensitive nervous systems, and I think at that age those systems were like a superpower we hadn't learned to harness yet. We were just becoming aware of the world but didn't yet know how to process it, only how to be affected by it.

What stands out most to me is how I learned, even then, that anxiety, fear, and worry impact us physically. They are not just in our minds; they are in our bodies. The physical effects of long-term worry include suppression of the immune system, digestive disorders, muscle tension, short-term memory loss, and premature coronary artery disease.[1] (That list makes me immediately start to worry, which seems counterproductive. Ha!)

We might blame modern life for our anxiety and stress, but apparently humans have struggled with remaining inwardly calm for a long time, whether or not they are creative introverts. Wise Solomon said,

> A peaceful heart leads to a healthy body;
> jealousy is like cancer in the bones. (Prov. 14:30)

Jealousy is really a form of worry, isn't it? We fear we may lose something (or someone) we value or never gain it at all. And that eats away at us not only mentally but also physically.

Fortunately, we don't have to let anxiety become destructive to our bodies. I'm a firm believer in working with a doctor (especially if you have *very* physical anxiety like panic attacks), finding a trustworthy counselor, and being intentional about reducing stress in our lives when we can.

There are also simple, short-term techniques we can use that focus specifically on our bodies. We experience anxiety when our fight-or-flight system is triggered. To return to a more peaceful state, our bodies need to turn off that system again. I've tried a variety of techniques for this, but the only one that seems to work well for me is box breathing.

Let's try it together . . .

Sitting upright, breathe in through your nose for a count of four until your lungs are full.

Hold that breath for a count of four.

Breathe out for a count of four until your lungs are empty.

Hold your lungs empty for a count of four.

Repeat until you feel your body begin calming down (for me, it takes about three rounds).

Studies have shown "intentional deep breathing can actually calm and regulate the autonomic nervous system . . . reduce stress and improve your mood."[2]

Sometimes I forget I'm a human being living in a human body. I try to make every answer to every problem superspiritual. But then I remember the story of Jesus raising a little girl, who was maybe about the same age I was when I hid in the nurse's office, from the dead. As soon as she comes back to life, Jesus says, "Give her something to eat" (Luke 8:55). He attends to the spiritual while not overlooking the physical. In doing so, he gives us an example to follow.

Because of the nervous system I have (which is also related to a lot of my strengths), I will likely always struggle in some way with anxiety. But what I've discovered through the years is that I'm no longer at its mercy.

Dear Anxiety, I'm all grown up now, and you are not the boss of me.

God, you formed every part of me, including my fight-or-flight response and nervous system. Help me not to feel shame or guilt over my anxiety but instead to bring everything I feel and all I experience to you. Show me how to deal with my struggles in a way that encompasses every part of me—spiritual, emotional, mental, and physical. Amen.

What helps you feel calmer? Make a list of at least three things so you can refer to it next time you feel anxious.

MY MIND HAS ALWAYS BEEN WIRED TO THINK A LOT. I live with a constant flow of thoughts, ideas, possible scenarios, potential conflicts, distractions, problems, and creative solutions. But slowly worry can creep in, and before I know it, pressure rises in my chest, tension builds in my shoulders, and my brain won't shift gears. . . . But we don't have to live that way. God wants to provide what we need.

RENEE SWOPE

8

get your goliaths

"Don't worry about this Philistine," David told Saul.
"I'll go fight him!"

                                                    1 Samuel 17:32

I first read the story of David and Goliath in a children's book
with bright illustrations and rhyming words. Since then, I've
heard it in sermons and corporate speeches and seen it depicted
in museum art and used as a sports metaphor. The focus is always the dramatic moment when a shepherd boy takes down
a champion giant with only a sling and a stone.

But this morning I noticed a phrase that comes before the
movie-worthy moment of victory happens. David says to King
Saul, "Don't worry" (1 Sam. 17:32). He doesn't say, "There's
nothing to worry about." He doesn't dismiss or minimize what's
happening. But he also doesn't get stuck in "standstill worry"
like the other soldiers.

Pastor Will van der Hart and psychiatrist Rob Waller, authors of *The End of Worry: Why We Worry and How to Stop,* would call David's attitude "solvable worry."

> Solvable worry is typically about problems that are currently happening and have a solution that is required now or at some point in the near future. It is often about a clearly understandable problem, one we would all be anxious about. Solvable worry has concrete characteristics and is authentic in that the mind is seeking out a resolution to a problem that provokes appropriate anxiety.[1]

Solvable worry prompts us to create a plan, and David gives us an example of how to do so.

- *Assess the threat.* "David asked the soldiers standing nearby, . . . 'Who is this pagan Philistine anyway, that he is allowed to defy the armies of the living God?'" (1 Sam. 17:26).

- *Reflect on what has worked in the past.* When Saul questions his ability, David tells him how he has defended his flock by fighting predators. He says, "I have done this to both lions and bears, and I'll do it to this pagan Philistine, too" (v. 36).

- *Evaluate the available resources.* David tries on Saul's armor but refuses it because it doesn't fit. Instead, he chooses five smooth stones, "then, armed only with his shepherd's staff and sling, he started across the valley to fight the Philistine" (v. 40).

- *Focus on truth and give the situation to God.* David says to Goliath, "You come to me with sword, spear, and javelin, but I come to you in the name of the LORD of Heaven's Armies. . . . This is the LORD's battle, and he will give you to us!" (vv. 45, 47).

- *Take clear and decisive action.* "As Goliath moved closer to attack, David quickly ran out to meet him. . . . So David triumphed over the Philistine with only a sling and a stone" (48, 50).

When fear taunts us, it can seem the most important question is, "How do I stop worrying?" But a more effective one is, "How can I start winning?" We need the whole story of David and Goliath. We need to understand how to make a brave, practical plan. Because giants and worry still can't stand in the face of obedient action.

God, thank you that I never have to let worry keep me from victory. When I feel stuck in fear, give me wisdom to evaluate the situation, create a plan, and take the next step of obedience. You are the One writing all of my story. Amen.

What's one thing you're worried about today? Make it as specific as possible: identify your Goliath. Then, using David's steps above, create a plan for taking obedient action.[2]

_____

_____

_____

WHATEVER GIANT WE'RE BATTLING MIGHT BE BIG—
but it's not bigger than Jesus.

LOUIE GIGLIO

9

optimize . . . or not

I am certain that God, who began the good work within you,
will continue his work until it is finally finished on the day
when Christ Jesus returns.

Philippians 1:6

I scroll through my social media accounts one evening just to see how many "shoulds" I can find at one time—whether directly stated or implied. I should follow a particular type of diet. I should declutter my home. I should go on a weekly date night with my husband. I should update my wardrobe. I should spend time with God by using a certain system. All these shoulds come with the promise that if I do as I'm told, my life will be happier. But is this actually true?

I did this experiment with my social media feed after reading an article titled "Optimize Now: The Never-Ending Pursuit of the Perfect Lifestyle." The author, Emily Lehman, explains that we live in an age of productivity guilt and optimization obsession. We're constantly trying to improve our lives, and in doing so we are, ironically, making them worse. Lehman says, "We get into a cycle of constantly 'fixing'—from our mental health to our cleaning supplies, there's always something to fix, with the ideal horizon constantly receding."[1]

A friend and I had brunch just after the new year. We're dreamers and goal-setters. But as she listed all the ways she wanted to change her life in the next 365 days, she didn't look inspired and motivated. She looked overwhelmed and discouraged. Her extensive list made me feel tired just hearing it. I looked at my lovely, kind, smart, successful friend and said, "You and I act like anything less than the ideal we have in our minds is failure, and it's not. Maybe what we need this year is to not be so hard on ourselves."

I grew up in a church that struggled with legalism. I learned to identify legalism by recognizing this formula: "You must _____ or _____ will happen." You must read your Bible every single morning or God will be mad at you. You must show up at church every time the doors are open or your life won't be blessed. It's a language of guilt and fear, not love and grace. It took me a long time to get free from it. But lately I find myself surrounded by it again—it's just that this time I'm not in church.

You should use this color scheme in your home or no one will want to spend time there. You should do this exact exercise program or you will never be healthy and happy. You should never watch television or you'll become a lonely recluse.

It doesn't matter if it's religious legalism or secular legalism, the underlying message is the same: optimizing everything is the only way to live. When we give in to this message, no matter the source, we place ourselves under law instead of grace.

Yes, we can make progress, learn, and grow. But if what we thought would improve our lives has become an obstacle to our peace and joy, then it's time to let it go. True transformation comes not from working *on* ourselves but from giving ourselves fully to the God working *in* us. "I am certain that God, who began the good work within you, will continue his work until it is finally finished on the day when Christ Jesus returns" (Phil. 1:6).

God, you have freed us from shoulds and invited us into a life of joy. When we're tempted to place ourselves under pressure, bring us back to the covering of grace. We entrust ourselves to the work you are doing in and through us. Amen.

What shoulds have you placed on yourself? List them, release them to God, and receive his grace in their place.

_____

_____

NOT EVERY good thing is a God thing.
PRISCILLA SHIRER

10

making friends with frustration

So let's not get tired of doing what is good. At just the right time we will reap a harvest of blessing if we don't give up.

Galatians 6:9

At the end of a long workday, a text appears on my phone. It's from someone in my mastermind group. "Today felt clunky," she says. It's an odd word yet one I can relate to—even in that very moment. I imagine you can, too, especially when trying to learn something new. My little mastermind group exists so we can challenge each other to grow, step out of our comfort zones, and learn and do hard things. Sometimes this is exciting and we have progress to celebrate. Other times, like this one, the process of moving forward feels slow and awkward.

I went on a walk later and listened to a podcast. A guest trained in neuroscience came on to give advice to graduates. He said, "Get comfortable, and even appreciate, feeling frustrated and confused."[1] This, more than anything else, had influenced his success, and he believed it would do the same for others.

This seemed like odd advice, but he went on to explain that confusion and frustration are the emotions we experience when the brain is rewiring itself. Our brain is very efficient and creates neural pathways when we do or think something repeatedly. These pathways are like roads that let us do what we need to do without thinking much about it. For example, we don't have to put a lot of mental effort into brushing our teeth.

When we learn, try something new, or push beyond our comfort zones, new pathways are required. Our brain always protests at first because this takes much more mental effort. We experience resistance in the form of confusion and frustration. This is the point when a lot of people give up. The solution, it turns out, is learning to recognize confusion and frustration in these moments as positive signs of progress.

The podcast said we need to tell ourselves, "It's okay. This is just me growing and adapting and learning. It's totally normal, and if I just keep going, eventually those connections will form, eventually the pathways will solidify."[2] When we persevere and let those pathways form, we will eventually experience an aha moment when we start to really grasp whatever it is that we're trying to learn or trying to do.

The apostle Paul said, "Suffering produces perseverance; perseverance, character; and character, hope" (Rom. 5:3–4 NIV). I've always thought of this in terms of external physical suffering, but I think it applies to the pain of personal growth too. Perseverance is pushing through even when it's hard and uncomfortable. Character means those efforts change who we are. And hope happens because we can see possibilities in the future where we couldn't before.

All of this means that when we have a "clunky" day—one where we don't make as much progress as we'd hoped, when we feel inadequate for what we're trying to do, when we can't quite seem to understand, when nothing really goes as planned—we can see it as a sign not of failure but of moving forward. In those moments, it's tempting to criticize ourselves or give up. Instead, we can recognize that we are doing hard work.

We are living with courage.

We are choosing to grow.

We are doing so much better than we know.

God, in the moments when I feel like giving up, help me choose perseverance. In the times when I want to criticize myself, bring me back to grace and your extravagant love. On the days when it seems like I'm failing, remind me that I'm fighting and you have promised victory in the end. I want to learn, grow, and move forward with you for a lifetime. Amen.

What's a time when you experienced confusion and frustration that eventually led to learning and growth (example: understanding something new in school, starting a new job, creating a healthy habit)?

_____

_____

_____

PERSEVERANCE IS GOOD, but that doesn't mean it's easy.

REBECCA HASTINGS

11

keep your pace

Let us run with perseverance the race marked out for us, fixing our eyes on Jesus, the pioneer and perfecter of faith.

Hebrews 12:1–2 NIV

My feet hit the pavement in a slow, steady rhythm. I am not fast. I am not graceful. But I like how stress rolls off me along with the sweat from my forehead, the way my favorite songs match the beat of my heart, and the satisfaction of discovering I'm capable of more than I first thought.

The sky spreads blue above me, and I'm content. Then I see another runner with a smooth, speedy stride I can hardly fathom, and suddenly I feel like I'm not doing anything right. My peace and contentment vanish. Have you ever felt the same?

You love the home you have until you see someone else's fancy renovation.

You're happy with your marriage until you watch a romantic movie.

You think your personality is just fine until you read your friend's witty posts on social media.

Your job brings you joy until someone else gets a raise and promotion.

We can so quickly shift from focusing on "the race marked out *for us*" to comparing ourselves with someone else (Heb. 12:1 NIV, emphasis added). God invites us to fix our eyes not on those around us but on the Savior who has gone before us. If we're focusing on a path besides our own, let's make sure it's the one that led to the cross. Because that changes everything.

Instead of what we don't have, it reminds us of all we've received.

Instead of how we don't measure up, it reminds us of the limitless grace that's ours.

Instead of self-pity, it gives us a reason to lift our hands and hearts in praise.

The path to the cross enables us to "not grow weary and lose heart." It helps us keep pursuing God's best for us and protects us from distraction. It also reminds us that the journey we're on is not about competition but completion. These days when I try to be like someone else, I go back to a phrase someone shared with me long ago: "Not my race, not my pace."

As the fast runner passes me, I repeat this in my mind. Soon Ms. Speedy Feet is out of sight. I wonder where she's going, then remember I'm headed home to where I belong—to the place where I'm loved as I am. Isn't that what really matters?

I so easily forget this truth: When I choose someone else's path, I also choose their destination. What God has for someone else may look good, but only his will for my life is truly best. I don't want to miss out on what God has prepared for me—even if sometimes I'm a little slower and less graceful getting there.

God, thank you for the path you have prepared for me and the Savior who has gone before me. I choose not to compare and instead to focus on pursuing you. I will keep my peace. I will honor my pace. I will trust that what you have ahead for me is best. Amen.

When are you tempted to compare? What helps you fix your eyes on Jesus and stay focused on the path he has for you?

_____

_____

_____

WE SET OUR EYES ON THE FINISH LINE TOGETHER. Some days we run; other days we kneel. Finishing well and leading our people to God's glory is the goal.

DORINA LAZO GILMORE-YOUNG

12

come, Lord

Come, Lord! The grace of the Lord Jesus be with you.

1 Corinthians 16:22–23 NIV

I pull into a hospital parking lot on a cool fall morning. Leaves crunch beneath my feet as I walk to the entrance. I find "Intensive Care Waiting Room" on the directory, ride an elevator, and find my friend. She offers me a weary smile and a doughnut from a box sitting on a table next to her. I take a seat instead of the doughnut and wrap my arms around her. What do you say in moments like this one?

A few days ago, she'd been diagnosed with breast cancer, a recurrence of a battle she fought (and won) almost thirty years before. Then, in the same week, her healthy, active husband had a heart attack no one saw coming. A double bypass followed. The surgery went well. He would go home. But for now, we waited.

I'd woken up long before the sun rose that morning. With a heavy heart, I thought of my friend. One word kept coming to mind: *Maranatha*. I knew it originated in Scripture but couldn't recall where it appeared or even what it meant. When I started researching, I found *Maranatha* is translated "Come, Lord!"

"Shalom" is the traditional Jewish greeting. But early Christians greeted each other with "Maranatha" instead. It's a one-word prayer. And, yes, the ultimate desire behind it is for Jesus to come back and take us Home. But it means much more than that too.

I said "Maranatha" over and over as I prayed for my friend.

Come, Lord, into the middle of these hard circumstances.

Come, Lord, with your power and peace.

Come, Lord, with your comfort and strength.

Yes, God is always with us, but I've had moments—and I imagine you've had them too—when he feels *especially* present. As I sat with my friend in the waiting room, she described how she felt that way in her husband's hospital room.

She said, "None of this makes sense. We know that. Yet I trust there's something deeper I don't see. Something in the deep, waiting for me and those I love. This is how God works, and for all of you saying, 'Where is God in all of this?' my answer is that he's right here—over, under, in front, behind, and around us."[1]

When our world falls apart, plans crumble, and our hope flutters like a tattered flag, God has not left us. He's a God not of distance but devotion, not of neglect but infinite nearness, not of apathy but affection so great he gave everything for us.

I don't know how my friend's story will unfold in the next few months, but I'm certain she won't face it alone. Whatever you're going through, that's true for you too. God is present in the hardest moments of our lives. He's there in the dark when we whisper prayers for those we love. He's with us in the waiting rooms.

Come, Lord, into whatever the future holds.

God, sometimes life doesn't turn out the way we'd hoped or planned. Thank you that we can trust you are with us and for us even in those moments. You will never leave us or forsake us. We will never face anything alone. We trust you now. We trust you always. Maranatha. Amen.

What's a hard moment in your life when you sensed God's presence and care?

_____

_____

IN THE MIDST OF BROKEN THINGS, broken lives, broken bodies, broken relationships, we can stand firm in the hard and call out to others, *Come! God has not abandoned you. Come stand with us. Come lie down and rest. Come, just come. I can hold on for the both of us right now. Though the way is hard, our greatest hope is unchanging. Our hope is sure and lasting. Jesus is coming again, and nothing can separate us.*

ELIZABETH MANLEY

13

going dormant

The righteous will flourish like the date palm [long-lived,
*   upright and useful];*
They will grow like a cedar in Lebanon [majestic and stable].
*   Planted in the house of the LORD,*
They will flourish in the courts of our God.

Psalm 92:12–13 AMP

We have two "horse apple" trees behind our house. They're spindly, like teenagers after a growth spurt. The fruit they produce is bright green, covered in bumps, and inedible. When we first moved in, we talked about removing them and planting something more splendid—an oak or a maple. But I've come to love our awkward pair of trees.

In spring, robins build nests in their branches. In summer, the trees provide shade. In fall, their leaves turn lovely and vibrant. In winter, their bare arms hold snow. I've watched the seasons of their lives, and it has made me think about mine.

The book of Psalms compares those who love God to trees. I understood the parts of the metaphor that involved growth and bearing fruit. But I'd missed an essential element of every tree's life: dormancy. When a tree goes dormant, it releases its leaves, slows its growth, and produces no visible fruit for a time.

This seems wasteful to me. Why not have trees bear fruit all year long? Isn't dormancy optional? When I researched this question, I discovered "it's possible to force a tree to evade dormancy if you keep it inside and with a stable temperature and light pattern. However, this is usually bad for the tree. It's natural for trees to go through dormancy cycles, and the lifespan of the plant is dramatically decreased if the tree isn't allowed to go dormant for a few months. Trees have winter dormancy for a reason, and it's best to just let them run their course as nature intended."[1]

I've read that quote dozens of times since I found it—because it speaks to something within me. We *all* need seasons of dormancy. Maybe we've gone through a time of great growth. Perhaps we're preparing for challenging circumstances. We might need to release what's no longer serving God's purposes for our lives.

Whatever the reason, dormancy can feel like a failure rather than a necessity. Shouldn't we produce more, try harder, keep doing what we've always done? It's possible to force a human to evade dormancy too, but it's hard on our souls. We become weary and depleted. The quality of the fruit in our lives suffers.

We, like the trees, have our seasons. It takes courage to slow down. It takes guts to let go. It is a brave thing to focus only on what's essential. But if God is inviting us into dormancy, we can trust it will not last forever. There will be growth again. "[Growing in grace] they will still thrive *and* bear fruit *and* prosper in old age; they will flourish *and* be vital and fresh [rich in trust and love and contentment]" (Ps. 92:14 AMP).

My horse apple trees will live about seventy-five years. According to life span statistics, you and I are likely to do the same. Sometimes we live like there is only one season—the one we're in now. But there are many, and they're all necessary, all beautiful in their own way, and all ordained by a loving God.

God, you are the Creator of the trees and of my heart. You know the needs of both. Give me the wisdom to embrace all you have for me—times of growth, times of rest. Thank you that my value to you isn't determined by what I produce. Seasons change, but I am always loved the same. Amen.

What season of life are you in right now? What is God teaching you in it?

_____

_____

_____

AS THERE ARE PATTERNS FOR OUR DAYS, there are also ingrained patterns for our seasons. Summer gives way to fall and fall gives way to winter and winter to spring and so on, indefinitely.

What do these patterns tell us? Why did God write the pattern of our days and seasons into the DNA of the world? They are physical reminders of a deeper reality; *they display God's pattern of redemption.*

CHRISTINE HOOVER

14

more than a cliché

Why, my soul, are you downcast?
  Why so disturbed within me?
Put your hope in God,
  for I will yet praise him,
  my Savior and my God.

Psalm 42:5 NIV

My grandparents owned a Christian bookstore in a little South Texas town with palm trees on the street corners. This perpetually sunny place felt like paradise to me, a young writer and insatiable reader. I collected whatever books caught my eye, dragged them to the back room, curled up in a worn leather chair, and feasted on words.

Their store also meant I had access to a variety of Christian paraphernalia. This was the 1980s, and I made sure to stock up on items like bumper stickers that said, "Solar powered by the Son." I slapped them on the binders I carried to school and toted them around as if I were in a positivity parade.

While the stickers themselves were harmless (and amused my friends), I also picked up a tendency to slap spiritual clichés on my heart, especially when I was hurting. I thought I had to keep a smile on my face at all times or people wouldn't like Jesus. I'm not quite sure where I got this notion. It wasn't from my family, but it stuck with me through my teenage years and into adulthood, where it certainly contributed to my depression and anxiety.

It wasn't until my early twenties that I started to get free, when grace became more than something I sang about and, instead, grew into something I clung to with all I had. Many factors contributed to this healing—counseling, dear friends, churches that believed in love rather than legalism. I also found great comfort in the Psalms, which were filled with raw honesty about how hard it can be to live in this world even when you have faith. Psalm 42:5 became one of my favorite verses.

> Why, my soul, are you downcast?
>   Why so disturbed within me?
> Put your hope in God,
>   for I will yet praise him,
>   my Savior and my God. (NIV)

This morning I became curious about how Psalm 42 ends. I hadn't read it in a while and felt entirely surprised to find it closes by repeating *exactly* the same words as the verse above. I'd expected a bow tied neatly around a truth, a declaration that all was now well, an upbeat and catchy phrase.

But, no, the psalmist still has the same questions, stresses, and struggles. This is comforting to me because it reminds me all over again that I don't have to live with bumper-sticker faith. God isn't expecting me to get over anything. He isn't requiring me to find the perfect cliché that will make my hurt go away. He isn't uncomfortable with the in-between, the places where we are not yet healed.

Another Psalm I love says,

> But you, LORD, are a shield around me,
>   my glory, the One who lifts my head high. (3:3 NIV)

When we are downcast, we don't have to lift ourselves up; *God will do it*. He is so much more tender with us than we are with ourselves. He will give us time and space, all we need. He doesn't snap up our head like a general rebuking a soldier but rather lifts up our head like a father does a child with tears streaming down her cheeks. That is why we can say with the psalmist, "I will put my hope in God," even in our worst moments, our hardest times.

I wish I could go back to my younger self with her bumper-sticker binders. I'd tell her, "First, stop using so much Aqua Net hairspray. Also, you don't need to try so hard or live up to all those clichés. You will always and only need one little word—*grace*."

*God, thank you that you don't expect me to just "cheer up"
or force myself to get over anything. Instead, you enter the
hard places with me. You are so patient with me. You lift
my head not by force but with great gentleness and care.
Help me extend the grace you've so freely given me to others. Amen.*

What's a phrase you tend to say to yourself that isn't
grace-filled (example: "Get over it")? What's a truth you
can replace that cliché with today (example: God isn't
rushing my healing)?

_____

_____

_____

ONE OF THE GREATEST GIFTS we can give someone . . .
is bearing witness to their pain. Not coming with neat answers
wrapped in tidy Christian clichés. Just come. Show up so a friend
is not alone in the question-asking, faith-wrestling, soul-wrecking
agony.

BECKY KEIFE

15

you are seen and known

Search me, O God, and know my heart;
test me and know my anxious thoughts.

Psalm 139:23

I lost a spool of gold satin ribbon. I searched my basket of craft supplies, my closet shelves, the back seat of my car—where I did discover granola bar crumbs, lip gloss, and a church bulletin from six months ago. I'd bought the ribbon to make a sash for a bridesmaid dress I'd worn in the recent wedding of a friend (by make, I mean ask someone else to tie the aforementioned ribbon in a bow). I'd planned to use the leftovers for Christmas packages. But I finally threw my hands up and consigned the spool to the unknown space where missing socks must also go when they disappear from the dryer.

Months later I pulled open a drawer in the cubby area close to our back door. This area has hooks for coats and purses, a long bench, and two drawers that normally go unused. But when I opened one, it all came rushing back to me. I'd been having a group of people over and didn't have enough time to properly clean up. So I grabbed whatever I could, shoved it all into this drawer, and promptly forgot about it. This is not the first time I've committed such a crime. I've been known to shove dirty dishes into the oven, kick wayward shoes out of sight under the bed, and push dust bunnies into dark corners as if I'm herding cattle.

I can do the same with what I consider unsightly in my heart. Struggles, stresses, ugly attitudes, worries, imperfections. I don't want anyone to see—what would they think of me? I don't want God to see either. I'd better clean myself up and be presentable or risk losing his favor. So it surprises me when the psalmist extends this invitation:

> Search me, O God, and know my heart;
>> test me and know my anxious thoughts. (Ps. 139:23)

This is the opposite of hiding. Instead, it's a request to be searched. Why would anyone want this?

As I ponder the answer, I think back to my lost spool of ribbon. What if someone in my home had known exactly where it was the whole time? Instead of wasting my energy and efforts, I could have simply asked, "Will you help me?" The search would have soon been over. It seems I'm hesitant to do the same with God because I don't consider what might be found to be like gold satin ribbon. Instead, I see it as shameful and unworthy— something to be kept out of sight.

I forget, so easily, that God wants to bring everything into the light. When he does, it's somehow transformed. The anxiety turns into faith. The fear becomes courage. The worry becomes trust. We don't ever need to be concerned about what he might find. First, because he already knows it's there. And also because there's nothing his love can't redeem.

I pulled the gold satin ribbon from the drawer and put it back where it belonged. I had plans for it. I could already see how useful all of it would be.

What if God feels the same when he searches you, searches me?

God, it's so easy to hide parts of who I am that I'm afraid for you to see. Instead, I ask, as the psalmist did, for you to search me and know my heart, test me and know my anxious thoughts. Then take whatever you find and transform it as only you can. I place all of who I am in your hands. Amen.

What's one thing you're tempted to hide from God, others, or yourself? Write it here as a first step to letting God reveal and heal it.

SOMETIMES, IF I'M NOT CAREFUL, I find myself wanting to find a shadow to hide from the darkness of my own soul. I want to cover up the imperfections that the light reveals, the brokenness, the scars and the failures. Then the voice cries out confidently, "I see you, I know you and I love you; there's no need to hide."

CAITLYN SNYDER

16

staying steadfast

Let your steadfast love, O LORD, be upon us,
even as we hope in you.

Psalm 33:22 ESV

In the center of my childhood backyard was a tetherball set, a tall white pole with a rope attached to it that had a ball on the end. My brother and I would take turns hitting that ball as hard as we could and watching the rope wind around the pole—spin, spin, spin.

On a recent stressful day, I prayed about an ongoing challenge in my life, and I kept picturing the tetherball set. I hadn't thought of it in years, and the memory felt a bit faded around the edges. One word also kept coming to mind: *steadfast*. It's not a word we use often these days. I mostly knew it from hymns and psalms. But I looked up the Hebrew meaning and learned that to be steadfast is to be "firmly fixed." Huh . . . just like the tetherball pole.

The apostle Paul told the Corinthians, a church surrounded by chaos, "My dear brothers and sisters, be steadfast, immovable"

(1 Cor. 15:58 CSB). Sometimes the most courageous, loving thing we can do is hold steady.

This is true when someone we love is battling an addiction and we must set boundaries instead of enabling. It's what we can do when a workplace is caught up in a swirl of stress and frustration even if it would be easier to give in to the griping and gossip. It's the position we can take when it feels like everything in our lives is changing without our consent.

Is this easy? Absolutely not. Will the people around us always understand? Not likely. Will we be tempted to act like the ball instead of the pole and spin, spin, spin? Quite possibly. Choosing to be steadfast requires grit and perseverance, bravery and great strength. It's far easier to just do something, *anything*, because at least then we feel as if we have some control. But realizing all we can really control is our own actions and choices can be a step toward freedom.

And, thankfully, we don't have to stand firm by ourselves. We're called to steadfastness because it reflects the heart and character of God.

> But this I call to mind,
>   and therefore I have hope:
> The steadfast love of the LORD never ceases.
>   (Lam. 3:21–22 ESV)

I don't know what happened to my old tetherball set. But today I'm grateful for the unexpected memory of it. Next time

I'm tempted to give in to the chaos around me, I'll picture that rusty, banged-up, resilient pole. I'll pray for the courage to be a little more like it, a little more like the God we can rely on to be steadfast forever.

God, I ask for the courage to be steadfast even in challenging circumstances. Give me the strength, peace, and resilience I need to stand firm. I will not let chaos pull me away from your plans for me. Thank you for your steadfast love that I can count on no matter what. Amen.

What's one way you've seen God's steadfast love in your life? What's one small way you can practice being steadfast today?

_____

_____

_____

LIKE A MOUNTAIN THAT CANNOT BE MOVED, God's presence is steadfast. . . . We may weep over what we've lost, struggle through our impossibilities. But—and this is important—we won't be alone in it. God is with us, *always*.

MICHELE CUSHATT

17

God will never leave you

God has said,
"Never will I leave you;
never will I forsake you."
Hebrews 13:5 NIV

We all know the stress of being hurt by another human. We've felt the shattering of a heart, the wounds of a careless word, the inner emptiness someone we love used to fill. These experiences can make us afraid when it seems as if the pain may happen all over again.

I felt that way recently when a friend became unexpectedly distant. The old anxiety crept up on me. What if I'd done something wrong and didn't know it? What if she'd found someone she liked better and no longer wanted me in her life? What if she silently slipped away and I never knew why? I kept trying to talk myself out of all these scenarios. It seemed a bit embarrassing to have such worries at this stage in my life, as if I was still a junior high kid waiting for someone to take the seat next to me at the lunch table.

But no matter how much I tried to dismiss these concerns, they remained—a gray cloud hovering over my day. I finally decided to pray (I'm slow with such things sometimes). I first asked God, "Will you promise me that this person I care so much for won't leave me?" I heard only silence in response. After asking several more times, it seemed I finally sensed this from him: "I can't promise you that this person won't leave you. But I promise that I won't."

I thought then of what Jesus went through on this earth. A dear friend betrayed him to be crucified. Another denied him multiple times. He knew what it felt like to be abandoned, forsaken, and disappointed by those closest to him. The hard reality of the world is this: we are fallible people, and even the best of us are capable of letting down those we love. There is no friendship immune to this possibility. No marriage without vulnerabilities. No family member who may not at some point treat us more harshly than a stranger. When we try, like I did, to put our trust in the perfection of people, then we are standing on shaky ground. But we can know, trust, believe, and fully rest our entire selves on the unconditional, unchanging love of God.

I also believe that because we are created for relationship, God will put people into our lives for each season. Looking back over my life, I could see that if one friend did drift away, another came along—if I had the courage to keep letting that happen.

Eventually I heard from my distant friend. All was well. She'd been in a busy season and missed me. I breathed a sigh of relief. It could have gone differently. Someday it still might.

The difficult thing about sharing this earth with each other is that we are all bulls in a china shop crashing into each other's hearts. The beautiful thing is that our God is a mender, ever-present to make us whole again. He will never leave or forsake us. This is what we can rely on, what we can forever trust.

God, you know what it's like to live in this world and be let down by those you love. When the same happens to me, please draw me close to you and remind me that I am never, ever alone. You are with me and for me in every moment. Give me the courage to keep loving despite the risks. Amen.

Who in your life needs to be reminded of your love for them today? Connect with them in some way and let them know you're there.

_____

_____

_____

THE ENORMITY OF HOW GOD LOVES US, protects us, pursues, welcomes, and seeks us out are so much more than we can imagine.

JENNIFER SCHMIDT

18

handling conflict

As iron sharpens iron,
*   so a friend sharpens a friend.*
            Proverbs 27:17

I'm allergic to conflict. Put me anywhere near an argument and my face turns pink, I sweat like I'm standing on the equator, and I start to hyperventilate. It doesn't matter if the conflict is happening within my family or on a television show where a fake judge is presiding over cases involving people who have clearly lost their minds. Take too many items to the express checkout line, and I won't confront you. Cut me off in traffic, and I'll watch you drive away. Look at me cross-eyed, and I might cry.

So when a friend came to me a few years ago to talk about a disagreement she was having with someone in her life, I completely surprised myself by saying, "Well, iron sharpens iron—that means sometimes sparks fly." I had never thought about this in my entire life. When this sort of thing happens, I tend to believe God is perhaps trying to tell me something. Later that day, I considered that my attitude toward conflict might have been misguided.

In particular, I remembered a class I took in college called "Communication and Conflict." The one thing I can still recall from that entire semester is learning that the couples most likely to split up are not those who fight a lot but those who *never fight at all*. Conflict, it turns out, is necessary in a healthy relationship. At the start of a conflict, there is an "I" and an "I," but when done successfully, by the end there's a "we."

This doesn't mean all conflict is created equal. John Gottman, a psychologist and researcher, has studied conflict for decades. He can predict with stunning accuracy and speed which relationships will last and which will not. Based on years of observations, he has come up with four stages of conflict.[1] The first is simply criticism. ("You left your dirty laundry on the floor again. Can you please pick it up next time?") This is focused on behavior and often accompanied by a request. The next phase is contempt. ("You're such a slob.") It's at this point that conflict becomes destructive, because it's no longer about behavior and has become an attack on someone's character. Next comes defensiveness, usually a response to contempt. ("Who are you calling a slob? You're a total mess.") When contempt and defensiveness become a pattern, it leads to stonewalling, an emotional cutoff between the two people involved. If stonewalling really sets in, it's very difficult for the relationship to recover.

It matters that we understand the good, bad, and ugly of how conflict works, because if we don't, then we can become people who settle for peace at any price. We hear "blessed are the peacemakers" and think it's the same as "blessed are the peace-*keepers*." But the two are very different. Making peace means honest communication, grace, compassion, openness about our wants and needs, empathy for the wants and needs of others, a willingness to be vulnerable, patience, and lots of respect. Peacekeeping often means stuffing our feelings, letting ourselves be taken advantage of, allowing harmful behavior to continue, and building up resentment.

I write in *Fiercehearted*, "I still hate conflict. But I have also come to see that it is not all 'bad.' That rough exterior hides gifts. Like showing us what we really want and who we really are. . . . My refusal to ever have conflict with others meant I was in conflict with myself."[2]

I still may not confront anyone in the grocery store line (I'm breaking out in hives at the thought), but I'm learning to speak up when it really matters. I'm learning to let iron sharpen iron, yes, and to watch the sparks fly. I'm learning the most valuable, beautiful peace is sometimes the kind that comes after a worthwhile battle fought for the sake of love.

God, conflict can be hard and scary—it can also be destructive. Yet during your time on earth, you never shied away from it. You show us how to have conflict that's about love,

not revenge; about compassion, not getting what we want; about speaking the truth with grace, not tearing each other down. Show us how to do the same. Amen.

How do you feel about conflict? What do you think is the difference between constructive conflict and conflict that destroys relationships?

_____

_____

_____

HERE ARE SOME GREAT QUESTIONS TO ASK WHEN WE'RE DEALING WITH CONFLICT OUT OF A DESIRE TO IMPROVE A RELATIONSHIP:

- Can you help me understand why you feel this way?
- Why don't we both agree to stick to the issue at hand and not pull in past issues?
- What is your desired outcome in this situation?
- How can we meet in the middle on this issue?

LYSA TERKEURST

19

it's only pie

*I tell you not to worry about everyday life—whether you have
enough food and drink, or enough clothes to wear. Isn't life more
than food, and your body more than clothing?*

Matthew 6:25

I scatter flour across parchment paper like snow in preparation
for placing a pie crust on it. I'm home in my kitchen, music
floating through the air along with the scent of the bacon we've
just had for breakfast.

My mama is to my left making her own pie. Hers will be
pumpkin. Mine will be apple. My crust has irregular borders and
lumps in various places like tiny mountains. I made it a few days
ago in a pie-making class. The instructor assured me it was fine,
lovely even, but I'm comparing it to the perfect circles I've rolled
out of cardboard boxes. I place another piece of parchment on
top of the crust and use a glass as a makeshift rolling pin. The
dough yields, flattening and spreading.

As I work, I remember what the baking class instructor kept saying to us: "It's only pie." She said this when her students first walked in wide-eyed and slightly terrified, as if we were going to learn to dismantle nuclear bombs rather than bake. She repeated it when someone added a bit too much flour or too little salt. She declared it when we folded our pie crusts, wrapped them, and got ready to carry them home where we would complete our creations alone (gasp!).

This pie-making class is just one example of how I sometimes take life far too seriously. Yes, there are occasions for true distress, and I'd never dismiss those. I'm an advocate of crying the tears, punching the pillow, addressing the issue. But I can let myself get worked up over bad hair days and traffic, imagined mistakes or a single sentence in a conversation that happened months ago. Jesus said, "I tell you not to worry about everyday life—whether you have enough food and drink, or enough clothes to wear. Isn't life more than food, and your body more than clothing?" (Matt. 6:25). In other words, *it's only pie*.

My crust takes shape and I place it in a pie plate, then cover it with apples. I carefully cut the strips as I was shown and braid them into the lattice top we learned in class. I feel like a little girl braiding a friend's hair, making the strips go under then over until the work is complete. When I'm finished, it certainly looks as if a child might have done it—the strips are unevenly spaced and slightly lopsided. I slide it into the oven anyway.

The next day my pie is devoured by forkfuls. My family declares it good and has seconds. I stressed myself out for nothing.

When I'm complimented, I smile and say those familiar words in a different way. "Oh, it's only pie." I tell myself to remember that phrase, to tuck it into my heart like leftovers into the refrigerator. I want to bring it out again when I find myself anxious or concerned about what's small and inconsequential, when I'm tempted to hand over my joy to something entirely too tiny to be worthy of such a sacrifice.

After decades on this earth, I'm still learning to make pie. And I'm still learning to make peace with the little complications and annoyances of everyday life. But I will practice. I will be patient with myself. I will enjoy the good things that eventually come from the process.

God, you are the One who takes care of every detail of my life. Thank you that I don't have to worry about the little things because you are a big God who loves me. I release all that concerns me to you. Amen.

What's something small that sometimes tries to stress you out and steal your joy? Pause and tell our big, gracious, loving God about it.

_____

_____

YOU DON'T HAVE TO WORRY ANYMORE. Why? Because of Jesus. That's why. He's got this. And He's got *you*.

JENNIFER DUKES LEE

20

you can fight back

Overwhelming victory is ours through Christ, who loved us.

Romans 8:37

I show up to a gym that smells like tanning lotion and citrus air freshener. A couple of weeks ago, a little sign advertising a new kickboxing class near the college I was attending caught my attention. I envisioned myself as something like the female version of Daniel in *The Karate Kid*. I'd be able to take down muggers in dimly lit parking lots, fight off bad guys wearing ski masks, save the world.

What I failed to consider is that my nature is inherently gentle. I rescue bugs and release them back into the wild. I cover my eyes during violent movie scenes. I like soft blankets and mugs of tea. Perhaps the instructor suspected all this when he eyed me suspiciously as I walked in the door.

The class itself is a blur. My mind is probably blocking it out so I don't have to relive the embarrassment. I only remember this one thing: I could not bring myself to fight back. My kicks looked more like awkward dance moves. After the class, I shrugged, bought some pepper spray at the store, and went back to doing step aerobics.

But I thought of the class again this morning when familiar phrases kept coming at me like punches. When I'm very tired or stressed out, my inner critic uses words like *disappointment, failure, bad*. I've learned to ignore these attacks or distract myself until they stop. But today that didn't feel like enough.

I felt like I was in that kickboxing class all over again. But this time I was in it to win. I was ready to fight back now. So when I heard each word, I threw back truth in return.

Disappointment.

Daughter of the King.

Failure.

Favored by God.

Bad.

Beloved.

I've found shame and guilt always try to hold me back from engaging in the battle. They try to tie my hands by telling me I deserve the accusations. After all, I'm not perfect. I fall short every day, no matter how hard I try. I should just take it.

But Jesus already took everything on our behalf.

> He was pierced for our rebellion,
>   crushed for our sins.
> He was beaten so we could be whole.
>   He was whipped so we could be healed. (Isa. 53:5)

In other words, Jesus didn't fight back *so that we can*. Not only that, we are promised that when we do fight back, we will win. The enemy's only hope is convincing us not to even engage but to stand there and take the blows. Because he knows, he *knows*, there is nothing stronger or more powerful than the God who lives within us and the truth he gives us.

I know now what I didn't back on that day I walked into the gym: We can be gentle and fierce all at once. We can feel weak and yet be strong. We can flunk kickboxing class and still be a mighty warrior when it matters most.

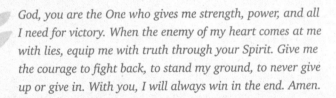

God, you are the One who gives me strength, power, and all I need for victory. When the enemy of my heart comes at me with lies, equip me with truth through your Spirit. Give me the courage to fight back, to stand my ground, to never give up or give in. With you, I will always win in the end. Amen.

What does your inner critic say to you? What's the truth that will combat those attacks?

_____

_____

WHILE WE MAY BE TINY, we can fight big when God is on our side.

ANNA RENDELL

21

lean into love, not law

As pressure and stress bear down on me,
I find joy in your commands.

Psalm 119:143

I read the verse above in a coffee shop on an ordinary Thursday morning, a latte to my right and a little vase holding a handful of yellow daisies in front of me. It seemed a fitting setting for a spiritual aha moment. But I only scratched my head and thought, *God, I don't understand this at all.*

Maybe you've never had this experience, but it's not the first time I've come across a Scripture verse that makes no sense whatsoever to me. I might as well be reading it in the original Greek or Hebrew. Thankfully, we serve a God who's not intimidated by our curiosity or questions. So I stared off into space, past the yellow daisies, and did a bit of pondering.

At breakfast this morning, Mark and I had a conversation about a comment someone offhandedly made about us. Its intent wasn't unkind, but it smacked of religious judgment, and I was still struggling to shrug it off. Experiences like this are what make the psalmist saying, "I find joy in your commands" sometimes feel like a mystery to me (Ps. 119:143).

I've thought of commands as measuring sticks held in the hands of legalistic people. I've seen commands as sources of shame and guilt. I've imagined commands to be restrictive and harsh. As I consider all this, I realize those kinds of commands aren't actually what's being talked about here. Instead, they're human rules that have been made to look like gospel. What the psalmist is exclaiming about instead are the commands that come from God's heart.

Someone once asked Jesus, "Which is the most important command in the law of Moses?" (Matt. 22:36). Jesus replied, "'You must love the LORD your God with all your heart, all your soul, and all your mind.' This is the first and greatest commandment. A second is equally important: 'Love your neighbor as yourself.' The entire law and all the demands of the prophets are based on these two commandments" (vv. 37–40).

Suddenly my perspective on Psalm 119:143 shifts. The psalmist isn't saying, "As pressure and stress bear down on me, I find joy in your rules." No, instead, it seems the meaning is more like "As pressure and stress bear down on me, I find joy in your ways of love." When I'm experiencing times of stress and pressure, one of the most difficult parts is the uncertainty. I feel afraid, worried, and hurried—unsure of what will happen or if I will be able to handle it. I often don't know what to do. But

God's commands solve so much of this for us because they are unchanging, absolutely certain. They don't falter or fail.

When we find joy in God's commands, we choose to remember we are loved by him no matter our current circumstances or struggles. And we choose to extend that love to those around us regardless of their imperfections and challenges too. We even choose to love our messy, complicated selves in the middle of it all. It's easy to believe the goal of a command is correction. But, instead, it's connection, which is what we need most during life's hard times.

I'm reasoning with God today.

I'm wrestling with new truth.

I'm beginning to understand.

God, when I think of your commands only in terms of laws, remind me that they are, most of all, about love. In the middle of whatever I'm facing, your ways remain the same. Your character and heart bring me joy and security. I will build my life on who you are and how you care for me. Amen.

When you hear the word *command*, what words come to mind first? After reading this devotion, what new words can you add?

JESUS STANDS BY YOUR SIDE TO WHISPER, *You are worth it. You are worth the joy you long for. You are my beloved.*

BONNIE GRAY

22

yes, God delights in you

The very hairs on your head are all numbered. So don't be afraid; you are more valuable to God than a whole flock of sparrows.

Luke 12:7

It's snowing outside, delicate flakes falling from the sky like bits of cotton or lace. I live in a part of the country where this occurrence is rare enough to still be mesmerizing. I stand by one of the big windows in the kitchen, coffee mug in hand, to watch the show.

Only yesterday I refilled the bird feeder, and now it's surrounded by a flock of sparrows. A few finches join in, their wings adding flashes of yellow or red next to their plainer cousins. I feed these birds not because I must. No one compels me to haul home fifty-pound bags of sunflower seeds. I do so simply because these birds delight me. This makes me wonder if the God who also takes care of sparrows could possibly feel the same way about us. I go searching in Scripture, and I'm astonished to find these verses:

He led me to a place of safety;
he rescued me because he delights in me. (Ps. 18:19)

The LORD directs the steps of the godly.
He delights in every detail of their lives. (Ps. 37:23)

For the LORD delights in his people. (Ps. 149:4)

So often this isn't how I picture God feeling about me. It's easier for me to envision God tolerating me. God sighing and wondering when I will finally get it together. God being annoyed or frustrated like a parent whose child has just spilled a bowl of spaghetti all over a white tablecloth.

But as I watch these birds, I begin to understand this kind of delight. Because these birds aren't doing anything for me. They're not giving me compliments, mowing my lawn, or composing songs in my honor. No, my delight comes in just watching them *be*.

Oh, they are not perfect. Occasionally, one will deliberately knock another off the feeder, which results in shrieking and (literally) ruffled feathers. But there is still something about their innate *birdness* that I love. It's nothing impressive, really. They just eat and fly, build nests in the spring, hop around the yard, and occasionally do unspeakable things to the patio furniture.

I, however, can stress myself out trying to be good for God, showing off for him. But I wonder if the delight he feels in his people comes simply when we are being who he created us to be too—loving and working, sleeping and daydreaming, laughing and eating strawberry ice cream on a summer evening. It makes me think of how Jesus encouraged us to have faith like a child.

I think this sort of faith, perhaps more than anything else, is unselfconscious. A child has not yet learned to craft an image or hustle for recognition. For a brief number of years, a child simply *is*. He or she is like the sparrows, who know nothing other than to be true to who they are.

Thinking of the sparrows is both a challenge and a comfort to me on this snowy day. It makes me want to have the courage not to try so hard; it gives me the reassurance that I don't have to.

I watch the birds. A tenderhearted God watches me. He watches you too.

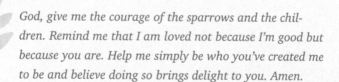

God, give me the courage of the sparrows and the children. Remind me that I am loved not because I'm good but because you are. Help me simply be who you've created me to be and believe doing so brings delight to you. Amen.

What does nature show you about who God is and who you are?

_____

_____

_____

_____

GOD SEES YOU NOW, and He delights in this exact moment you are in. Rest in His delight. Rest in the immeasurable rhythm of grace.

ALIZA LATTA

23

you don't have to work so hard

It is useless for you to work so hard
from early morning until late at night,
anxiously working for food to eat;
for God gives rest to his loved ones.

Psalm 127:2

I'm sitting on the couch, laptop in front of me, typing so fast it sounds like a machine gun, when my husband wanders into the room. He says something to me, and I reply with a vague "Hmm," which is my way of signaling "I'm busy and being productive. Please come back later." But he persists in his efforts to communicate with me, and I, such a kind and intentional wife, persist in mine to ignore him and carry on with my work.

I *know* better. I'm a licensed counselor and certified life coach. I've read the studies saying that the most powerful thing you can do in any relationship is turn *toward* the person trying to connect with you, not just physically but with your heart, mind, and attention.[1]

But I sometimes go back to a place I've been before—one of striving and hustle, trying too hard and working too long. I've been at my tasks for hours, barely taking a break to refill my coffee cup. My shoulders ache and so does my mind. I get to the point where I know I should have stopped hours ago, but I keep going.

Years ago, I often worked like this, and it took me to the brink of burnout. I wore my relationships thin. My faith felt like a burden. But I slowly learned to believe I was loved not for what I did but for who I am. I learned to have boundaries with my time and energy. I learned to rest. But, occasionally, I slip back into old ways.

Psalm 127:2 says it's useless for us to be *anxiously working*. I looked up the meaning of the original phrase, and anxiously working basically means "work that hurts." When God spoke the world into being, sculpted a man from clay and a woman from a rib, he made work holy and good. There is work that's sacred and life-giving. But there is another kind of work too—the kind that stresses us out.

I've found the difference between the two is that one comes from a place of fear and another from love. When I work to the point of exhaustion, it's almost always because I feel I have something to prove. My best efforts happen when, instead, I believe I'm already enough and remember success is about obedience, not outcomes.

I close my laptop and whisper a prayer. I find my husband and rest my hand on his shoulder. "I'm sorry," I say. "Tell me what you want me to hear."

A voice inside me tries to interrupt, saying, "You can't stop! You have more to do! You're going to fail if you don't get back at it right now." But I'm making a different choice this time. I listen to my husband. I listen to my truest self. I listen to the God who invites us not to labor but to let ourselves be loved.

God, thank you for inviting me not to hustle but to hear your voice telling me who I really am and that my worth isn't based on anything I do. Thank you for the gift of work. When I stray from your design for it and let fear take over, calm my anxiety and give me the courage to return to love. Amen.

How can you tell when fear is driving what you do? What helps you live and work in a different, better way?

_____

_____

_____

IF WE COULD FOCUS ON WHO—the Jesus in us and who He's making us into—then the DO will come without figuring or wondering. A beautiful life will unfold that we don't have to push or pry or agonize over.

STEPHANIE BRYANT

24

overcoming negativity

Fix your thoughts on what is true, and honorable, and right, and pure, and lovely, and admirable. Think about things that are excellent and worthy of praise.

Philippians 4:8

I walk along the edge of athletic fields, each one outlined in white chalk. There's a snow-cone truck at one end where the players, including my four-year-old nephew, will celebrate after their games. My nephew's favorite flavor has the word *dinosaur* in it and is bright red.

As I take a seat on the sidelines, I'm amused. One doesn't come to such events to witness athletic prowess but rather to be reminded of how there is more to playing than winning and losing. The players are currently involved in a variety of activities, including picking flowers, staring at birds, and chasing each other. There's a football that's occasionally noticed and pursued, but it doesn't seem to be the main attraction.

I played soccer when I was about the same age my nephew is now. I have only one memory from the entire season—kicking the ball down the field as everyone yelled, "Turn around! You're running the wrong way!"

Why do we often remember negative moments more easily than positive ones? Because of the negativity bias we all have. Our brains are wired to give more weight to negative experiences than positive ones and to hold on to them longer. As author Margie Warrell says, "We are Velcro for negative experiences, and Teflon for positive ones."[1]

The purpose of the negativity bias is to help us learn from our mistakes, pain, and failures. These lessons contribute to our physical and emotional survival. But left unchecked, our negativity bias can also increase our stress and anxiety. A number of studies have found a ratio that neutralizes the unwanted effects of our negativity bias. Whether in personal circumstances or relationships, we need to have five positives for every one negative.[2]

This ratio can sound challenging, and for years I struggled to incorporate this principle into my life. I finally landed on this: Every morning, the first thing I do is write a prayer listing at least five things I'm thankful for from the day *before*. I find my negativity bias can make it hard for me to be grateful in the moment. But with a bit of distance and the perspective of a new day, I can dig out the treasures I missed. I have two rules. First, nothing is too small to mention. Second, it's okay to repeat.

The apostle Paul told early believers to practice focusing on the positive too. He may not have known the term *negativity bias*, but the God who inspired him to write certainly knew this is a struggle for humans. In the verse at the start of this devotion, Paul offers another way to get to five positives. Ask, "What's one thing in my life right now that is . . . true, honorable, right, pure, lovely, admirable, excellent, worthy of praise?" If you come up with something for each of those words, you'll have eight positives (way to go, overachiever).

If these approaches don't work for you, just try something else. It may take some exploring and experimenting. The great news is that with time and practice, balancing your negativity bias will become automatic. It will be a lot of hard work and feel awkward or even fake at first. But eventually your brain will be retrained. If no matter what you do, you find it's impossible to think of anything positive, then you may be experiencing depression (I have). Talk with someone who can help, like a counselor or your doctor.

The referee blows the final whistle, and my nephew runs to us with a smile on his face even though his team has just experienced a defeat. His mind isn't fixed on his mistakes or what he could have done better. "Let's get a snow cone!" he says. As he tugs me toward the truck, I hope this is a moment we both remember.

God, thank you for how my negativity bias protects me and helps me learn. You gave it to me intentionally for my benefit. When it gets out of balance, help me refocus on what's true, honorable, right, pure, lovely, admirable, excellent, and worthy of praise. Your goodness is present in all of my days. Amen.

Try practicing the tool shared in this devotion from Philippians 4:8. List an answer for each word in this question: "What's one thing in my life right now that is . . . true, honorable, right, pure, lovely, admirable, excellent, worthy of praise?"

_____

_____

_____

GRATITUDE DIDN'T FIX MY PROBLEMS, but it helped me fix my eyes on Jesus.

LEE MERRILL

25

when life doesn't make sense

Don't worry about anything; instead, pray about everything.
Tell God what you need, and thank him for all he has done.
Then you will experience God's peace, which exceeds anything
we can understand.

Philippians 4:6–7

Almost two decades ago when we bought our first house, I rushed to the bookstore as soon as we signed the contract. I found the section labeled "Home Care" and perused the titles until I found a book several inches thick. I skimmed chapters about enticing topics like proper vacuuming technique, the best schedule for dusting, and how to clean grout with a toothbrush.

With great satisfaction, I carried the massive book to the register and toted it home. When I showed Mark, his response was a manly giggle. We'd been married for several years by now, and he said, "You already know how to take care of a house." I answered, "Yes, but I don't know *everything*."

This is the story of my life. If I'm facing uncertainty of any kind—whether a new situation, crisis, or unanswered question—I go into research mode. I find books. I search online. I survey friends. It's one of my go-to strategies for combatting stress. It actually works fairly well in certain circumstances, but the reality is that some issues we confront in life aren't so black-and-white. There's no manual for when everything starts falling apart, when nothing is going as planned. What do we do then?

In those moments, a particular phrase has become a great comfort to me. The apostle Paul says when we bring our needs and concerns to God, we'll experience his peace, "which exceeds anything we can understand" (Phil 4:7). This says to me that I don't need all the answers to still have peace. I experienced this kind of peace at the bedside of my grandfather as he slipped home to Jesus after battling cancer. I clung to it during our decade-long struggle with infertility. On this very day, Mark and I are waiting for a call that will shape our future, and we have no idea what will happen. But I know, *I know*, that whatever comes, it will be okay.

This kind of peace doesn't cancel out the blood, sweat, and tears. It doesn't mean we don't feel anger and sadness too. It's not a Pollyanna peace, where we pretend everything is dandy and we can make perfect sense of it all. No, this peace still gives us permission to feel all the feelings, to have all the doubts, to experience vulnerability and uncertainty. Not only do we not need to figure everything out, but we also don't need to make ourselves okay. God will take care of our hearts.

I never did use that housekeeping book. I set it on a shelf and promptly realized the perfect pictures and detailed cleaning plans did not match up well with real life. I don't have nice vacuum lines in my carpet. I've found dust bunnies gathering in corners as if they're planning anarchy. My grout has never encountered a toothbrush. Isn't that the way it goes?

We don't need a manual; we need Immanuel (a name for Jesus that means "God is with us"). It's his presence that makes the difference in our lives. It's his peace that will get us through whatever we may face.

God, thank you that you offer me peace even when I don't understand. I want the answers, but you give me what I truly need. Soothe my heart, calm my mind, help me bring all my questions and concerns to you because you love me more than I can even know. In Jesus's name, amen.

Think back to a time when you felt unsure or faced a hard situation that made no sense to you. How did God come through for you even then?

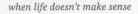

_____

_____

_____

MY QUESTIONS ARE NOT TOO BIG FOR [GOD]. As much as I'd like to conjure up my worth, I don't intimidate the Almighty, nor do my doubts. So I give them, *my doubts, my questions, my disbelief*, to him and choose to believe what I know to be true.

ALEXANDRA KUYKENDALL

26

guarding your heart

Guard your heart above all else.

Proverbs 4:23

We live in a neighborhood with a winding trail that runs through it. We've become familiar with the inhabitants along the way. There's a predictable line of bullfrogs on the shore of the first pond. An ancient, wise-looking turtle in the second. Four white ducks swim in the third, and someone recently constructed a tiny house for them.

There are also dozens of dogs. Tiny pugs and poodles. Several Labradors. A black-and-white Dalmatian and a speckled Great Dane. These dogs bark at us from behind fences, some with tails wagging and others with a ferocity that makes me glad we're separated by wood planks or iron posts. They're guard dogs, one and all, big or small. Unable to distinguish between a neighbor and a potential burglar, they attempt to chase off everyone and everything.

"Guard your heart above all else," wise Solomon said (Prov. 4:23). For so long, I pictured myself as the guard dog of my life. It was my duty to keep potential threats away. So anytime I felt fear or worry, stress or uncertainty, I sounded the internal alarm. I barked things at myself like "This is too scary" or "You're just going to get hurt." Yes, this worked, but it also meant I didn't always discriminate well between opportunities and actual danger. I, like a chihuahua yipping at a toddler on a tricycle, didn't necessarily have an accurate perspective.

Then I discovered that the phrase "guard your heart" appears again in the New Testament. It comes just after a passage that encourages us to bring all our worries and concerns to God. When we do so, "His peace will guard your hearts and minds as you live in Christ Jesus" (Phil. 4:7). What stands out to me most in this phrase is that we're not in charge of the guarding. Our role is staying in an intimate relationship with God and trusting him with everything we face. This means we don't have to live reactively, simply trying to defend our territory. We don't have to hide behind fences of our own making, pretending to be strong.

Instead, we can live in freedom and grace. We can take risks. We can reach out. We can dare to follow our dreams. Because God's peace will guard our hearts in the process. Each day we can wake up and say, "God, I trust you to take care of me."

Yes, we're to use wisdom and discernment, have healthy boundaries, and decide what to let in and out of our lives. But we don't have to feel helpless and confined. We're not at the mercy of whatever might come along. Even when life is hard, when the unexpected happens, when we feel vulnerable, we can know that we have a defender.

At the very end of the trail in our neighborhood is a wide-open field. Last time we walked by it, we paused to watch a golden retriever play with her owner. She didn't bark at us. She didn't even look our way. She had her eyes on the one she belonged to and trusted.

God, thank you for telling me to guard my heart. Thank you also that I don't have to do it on my own. I can bring everything that concerns me to you, and your peace will be my protection. I trust you with the most tender parts of who I am. Amen.

What do you need God's peace to protect your heart from today?

_____

_____

_____

TODAY, YOU ARE WORTH GUARDING, SWEET FRIEND.
Your heart—and you—matter to God.

SUZANNE ELLER

27

God will lift you up

When anxiety was great within me,
your consolation brought me joy.
Psalm 94:19 NIV

I walk through the restaurant door on a Saturday evening, hands tucked in the pockets of my sweater to guard them against the winter chill. The warm air inside instantly envelops me in the scent of bread and garlic, pasta and tomatoes—comfort served up on a plate. A waitress seats Mark and me in a booth with two of our dearest friends. We've been in each other's lives for almost twenty years. We've shared laughter and tears, triumphs and fears. Being with them always feels a bit like coming home. We tell each other we're the family we got to choose for ourselves.

We start, as usual, with any concerns from the week. We ask each other questions and find we're all in seasons of stress, dealing with extra pressure and disappointments. We hold nothing back. I've cried in front of these friends. They've seen me without makeup. They're not people to whom I say, "I'm fine."

The conversation continues as the waitress refills the bread basket and our entrees appear. Between forkfuls of deliciousness, the mood begins to lighten. We start showing each other silly photos on our phones. We tell stories of the ridiculous things we've done the past few days.

Then just as dessert is served, a slice of cake so big the four of us share it, my friend says to his wife, "Stop kicking me!" She looks startled, and I place my hand over my mouth. Because it's not her—it's *me* who has been unintentionally smacking his shin with the toe of my boot. I confess, and then we laugh so hard I have to grab the napkin from my lap to dab my eyes.

By the time we walk outside, I don't feel the chill the way I did when I walked in. This is the gift of being known, of being loved, of having dear friends. I thought of this dinner when I read King David's words,

> When anxiety was great within me,
> your consolation brought me joy. (Ps. 94:19 NIV)

The word *consolation* means "comfort received by a person after a loss or disappointment."[1] What if we think of God as a friend who consoles us, who wants to hear about our week and our worries, our doubts and discouragement, who will bring us from aching to joy?

There is a kind of comfort that sits with someone in the pit. This is good and necessary. But there is another kind that pulls you up out of it, that mysteriously takes you from tears to laughing so hard you cry. What if God wants to offer both to us? Yes, being compassionate and gracious, tender with our hearts, giving us all the time we need to grieve. But also bringing us gifts that delight and inspire us, that remind us that life is still beautiful, that surprise us with wonder.

Sometimes in the darkest moments of my life, it's not something big that gets through to my hurting heart. It's the crazy cardinal that insists on landing on our window ledge and peering into our living room as if he's watching television with us. It's the sound a baby makes when she's sleeping. It's the taste of a piece of dark chocolate. It's dinner with dear friends. All of these seem to whisper to my heart, "There is still good." I remember that's true and then I start looking for it, start believing again I can find it.

Yes, God is grand and beyond our understanding. But he is also our friend, the kind who would break bread with us on a cold winter evening, the one who knows exactly what will warm our hearts.

God, thank you that you are with me in the big moments, but you are also there in the small ones. When I am anxious, you are a friend who wants to bring me joy. Help me

recognize when you are doing something to delight me in the middle of my everyday life. Amen.

Think back over your day. What's one thing that made you smile or laugh? How can you see God's consolation in it?

_____

_____

_____

THE GIVER DOES NOT CHANGE. He is the same God who gave us the stars in the sky to light our way and His Son on Calvary to purchase our freedom. He still gives good gifts to his children. Do you see His eyes? They are smiling with delight. And His delight is for eternity.

STACEY THACKER

111

28

out of order

For God is not a God of disorder but of peace.

1 Corinthians 14:33

I used to have a closet that attacked me. In our first home, we didn't have much storage, and this meant a small closet outside our kitchen became a catchall space. I frequently shoved baking pans, cookbooks, scarves, gloves, and vacuum cleaner parts into it. I'd take a deep breath, close my eyes, and throw these items inside. This tactic worked for only so long. Soon the closet decided it'd had enough of my mishandling and randomly began throwing items back at me when I opened the door.

During this time, my life felt much like that closet. I was working full-time, going to graduate school, and trying to balance the responsibilities of being a grown-up with a home and a husband. I had a full-on case of perfectionism as well. Then God began healing my heart, slowing me down, and helping me realize my worth came not from how much I could do but from whom I belonged to. A funny thing happened during that process. The more I healed, the more I cleaned out that closet.

Author and podcaster Gretchen Rubin, who studies happiness and good habits, says, "I'm constantly surprised by the degree to which, for most people, outer order contributes to inner calm."[1] When we consider peace, we often think of the internal kind, but how we bring external order to our lives—whether it's an unruly closet or a scattered schedule—impacts us because we're spiritual *and* physical beings.

The Corinthian church seemed a bit like my closet when they got together. People talked over each other. Some used their spiritual gifts in ways that led to confusion. Chaos often broke out in services. The apostle Paul, their spiritual father, reminded them, "God is not a God of disorder but of peace" (1 Cor. 14:33). He gave them practical instructions about their gatherings: "Be sure that everything is done properly and in order" (v. 40).

At first, I didn't understand this directive. Why did order matter so much? But then I realized that when disorder is the norm, we're living *reactively*. This isn't in line with God's character, because he's proactive and purposeful.

After I finished cleaning out my unruly closet, I moved on to other areas of our house. It took over a year, but eventually I went through every corner of our home. When I finished, I felt like I could breathe again.

All of us have a different level of tolerance for disorder. I remember having a conversation with an artist friend of mine. She pointed out a picture in a magazine that showed a studio with paint, papers, and other creative tools scattered all over it. "I would love to have a place like this," she said with longing. I looked at her and said, "No way. I couldn't write with all of that going on around me." She replied, "That's because to write, you have to go inside yourself and block everything else out. I need to be able to look around and see inspiration everywhere."

While what works for each of us is different, we can all ask, "Is there disorder in my (life, home, office, calendar, family time, closet) that's impacting my well-being?" We've since moved to a different home, and I've tried to keep up my new habits. I no longer add so much to my closets. They no longer attack me. I will always make messes, and that's okay. But I'm grateful that I'm slowly learning to make peace too.

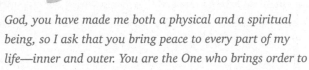

God, you have made me both a physical and a spiritual being, so I ask that you bring peace to every part of my life—inner and outer. You are the One who brings order to my chaos, who brings calm to my heart. Amen.

Is there disorder in your life that's impacting your well-being? If so, pick one small step (if it can be done in fifteen minutes or less, even better) to start bringing order to that area today. Note: Life is crazy sometimes—be sure to give yourself lots of grace in this process. This isn't about what's "good" or "bad" but what's doable and *best for you* in this season of your life.

I KNOW THINGS ARE STILL MESSY SOMETIMES, and that's okay, too. The messiness is what binds us together with all the other messy ones and shows us where we are needed most in this world.

JENNIFER RENEE WATSON

29

cast all your cares

Cast all your anxiety on him because he cares for you.

1 Peter 5:7 NIV

I stand at the edge of a pond, ripples across the waters mirroring those of my unsettled heart. I pick up a rock the size of my palm and place it in my hand, running my fingers across the surface worn smooth by time and troubles.

I bend over, pull my elbow back as if I'm a human slingshot, and throw the stone. It flies over the midnight-blue surface before skipping once, twice, and disappearing from view. I wipe the dust off my hands.

To "cast" our cares means more than just a tentative letting go—it's a hurling, tossing, complete release. This is the offer of God: to let him take our anxieties as the lake takes our stones, fully and completely. There is enough room to hold one care or a thousand. We can let them all sink beneath the surface of his endlessly deep love.

This releasing isn't a one-time event. It's a lifelong process. We can come to the shore of God's faithful love again and again, as often as we need. Yes, we are always welcome to give him whatever weighs us down so that we can continue our journey with freer, lighter hearts.

The question that can replace the space in our minds that our cares have occupied is simply this:

What is true right now?

God cares for me (1 Pet. 5:7).

He is always with me (Heb. 13:5).

He has promised to meet all my needs (Phil 4:19).

He will work everything together for good in my life (Rom. 8:28).

He . . . (finish this sentence with what your heart most needs to hear).

Instead of holding on to our cares, we can hold on to truth today. And that changes everything.

God, you are big enough to hold the world in your hands and loving enough to care about the smallest details in my life. When I'm anxious, you bring peace. When I'm afraid, you give courage. When I'm unsure, you provide confidence. I release my concerns to you now and entrust myself to your love. Amen.

What's a care you need to cast on God today? What's the truth you need to hold on to instead?

_____

_____

_____

JESUS WANTS US TO ENTRUST our concerns to Him, for He cares for us.

SUSIE LARSON

30

a quiet life

*Make it your goal to live a quiet life, minding your own business
and working with your hands, just as we instructed you before.*

1 Thessalonians 4:11

I didn't always make it until midnight to welcome in the new
year during my childhood. Perhaps that's why one New Year's
Eve stands out so vividly to me. I'd been allowed to spend the
night at a friend's house. She had a waterbed, which was the
height of coolness in those days. Another friend from school
came as well, and we sat cross-legged on a floral bedspread,
giggling about boys and watching the numbers on the clock
climb higher.

Just before midnight, we snuck out the front door and stood
in the middle of the street. The neighborhood seemed to be
asleep. The stars were scattered across the sky like diamonds
on velvet. Then the moment arrived—the New Year was here—
and the houses around us erupted in cheers. It felt like magic,

like the whole world had decided to put aside its grievances and celebrate.

That might have been when I fell in love with New Year's resolutions. I liked how that night felt like the first page of a blank journal, as if anything might be possible. I'm still a resolution junkie. I get a thrill out of dreaming up what might be. Yet in all the years I've made resolutions, this particular one has never been on my list: "Make it your goal to live a quiet life, minding your own business and working with your hands" (1 Thess. 4:11).

Our world would say it differently: "Make it your goal to live a loud life" or "Make it your goal to live a big life." We live in a culture where attention can seem like the most valuable commodity, where the way to success is to continually say, "Look at me!" The internet and social media make this easier, sure, but if Paul addressed the need for a quiet life all the way back in the early church, then that makes me believe this issue isn't new.

This morning I thought, *Maybe I've always misunderstood what the word* quiet *means in that passage*. So I pulled out my trusty word research tools and discovered that *quiet* in this context means . . . quiet. Peaceful. Still. As I pondered this, I thought of friends whose homes are bursting with kids, a woman at church who's an ER nurse, a former coworker who travels much of the year. What does a "quiet" life look like for them?

I recalled similar seasons in my life when, outwardly, there was a lot of noise. I felt anxious and stressed out, and I fell into striving. My inside was as loud as my outside. But recently I went to an event and felt entirely different. It was busy, sure. I was the keynote speaker, and the days were long. But I felt quiet on the *inside*. I've slowly learned a quiet life is about not simply the absence of noise but the presence of peace.

Paul goes on to encourage the Thessalonians to focus on "minding your own business and working with your hands" (1 Thess. 4:11). The principle behind this seems to be, "Focus your eyes and efforts on what God has specifically called *you* to do that's right in front of you." When my life gets loud, it's usually because I've started comparing. I've gotten away from who God has created me to be and what he has invited me to do. I've begun listening to the roar of insecurity rather than the voice of love.

That night standing in the street with my two friends, so much of our future was still ahead. We were barely at the beginning of our journeys to become the grown-ups we are today. I can still remember what that hush just before midnight felt like—how it seemed that anything could happen, anything might be, because our lives felt that way too. That's the kind of quiet I never want to outgrow, never want to give up or let go of . . . the kind of quiet that's filled with hope and expectancy.

God, you invite me to lead a quiet life, which is so differ-
ent from what the world around me says I must do. Give
me the courage to choose quiet, and show me what that

*means for me in this season of my life. I want to listen to
your love. Amen.*

What's one small way you can "make it your goal to lead
a quiet life" this week?

_____

_____

_____

THERE'S AN INVISIBLE WORLD that lives inside our bodies, the inner world of the soul. And this inner world needs our
attention, but it doesn't respond to programs, agendas, or hustle.
The soul responds to space, silence, and Jesus.

EMILY P. FREEMAN

31

helpful boundaries

May there be peace within your walls
and prosperity in your palaces.
For the sake of my family and friends, I will say,
"May you have peace."
For the sake of the house of the LORD our God,
I will seek what is best for you, O Jerusalem.

Psalm 122:7–9

My suitcase sits wide open on the closet floor. I pull shirts from hangers and toss them in as I think about the days to come. I'll be with a big group of people, and as an introvert, this can easily overwhelm me. I want to love well and serve faithfully, but I'm concerned I won't be up to the task. I quietly whisper a prayer for help, and it seems I hear this response: "Take care of yourself."

At first, I assume I must have picked up some kind of spiritual static. Surely this isn't what will benefit others most. But the more I pray, the more that phrase stays. So I shrug my shoulders and decide to give it a shot.

I've been with this group before, and I know days can be long, meals unpredictable, and activities surprising. I round up what I might need—granola bars for snacks, my own pillows for good rest, a puzzle and book for entertainment. Rather than being at the mercy of everyone present, I decide I'll state what I need. "I'm hungry, so I'm going to get something to eat" or "I'm worn out, so I'm going to take a nap." In other words, I decide to take responsibility for myself. I've avoided doing so in the past because I thought I might get criticized or seem uncooperative. But to my surprise, no one in the group seems to even notice, except perhaps for being relieved. Because I own my needs, they have one less person to worry about making happy.

Psychologists and authors Henry Cloud and John Townsend say in their classic book *Boundaries: When to Say Yes, How to Say No,* "Boundaries define us. They define *what is me* and *what is not me.* A boundary shows me where I end and someone else begins, leading me to a sense of ownership. Knowing what I am to own and take responsibility for gives me freedom."[1] We're to accept responsibility for what God has entrusted to us. According to Cloud and Townsend, this includes our feelings, attitudes and beliefs, behaviors, choices, values, limits, talents, thoughts, and desires, as well as our ability to give and receive love.

In other words, we are responsible for getting our needs and wants met. This seems like it could be selfish, but it's actually the opposite. If we don't take responsibility for getting our needs and wants met, then by default we're putting the burden for those on someone else. Doing so often leads to resentment, such as when I stood in the corner with my stomach growling and a scowl on my face because no one seemed to recognize I'd gone so long without eating that my blood sugar had gotten low. "May there be peace within your walls," writes the psalmist (Ps. 122:7). He was talking about the city of Jerusalem, the heart of Israel. But I think these words apply to our hearts and minds too.

This time around I didn't surrender my peace. It seems like such a little thing, but when I got hungry, I grabbed a granola bar. I stopped scowling and started serving. Similar scenarios happened throughout my time with the group. The experience felt entirely different.

Soon I found myself back home with my suitcase on the floor of my closet again. I unpacked my clothes and an unexpected new truth: taking care *of* ourselves helps empower us to care *about* others.

God, I want to love and serve well. Sometimes it seems this means not thinking about myself at all. But you have given me responsibility for particular parts of my life. Help me recognize what those are and do what's needed in those areas. Give me peace within my walls. In Jesus's name, amen.

What's one way you take care of yourself that helps you be able to care about others too?

_____

_____

_____

JESUS CALLS US TO LOVE our neighbor as ourselves. The key part of that calling is that we can only love others in our lives (our families, our neighbors, our coworkers, etc.) to the degree that we are taking care of ourselves. So to love well, and thereby *live well*, we must make a change to go from barely surviving to thriving.

JESSICA TURNER

32

being a peacemaker

But the wisdom from above is first of all pure. It is also peace loving, gentle at all times, and willing to yield to others. It is full of mercy. . . . Those who are peacemakers will plant seeds of peace and reap a harvest of righteousness.

James 3:17–18

Sometime in recent years it feels like the volume got turned up in our world. The internet in particular can feel like an angsty teenager blaring angry music with no concern for anyone else in the house. Social media is full of rants and arguments, strongly stated opinions and individual manifestos, subtle insults and divisive declarations. Stressful. I imagine you, like me, have sometimes wished for virtual earplugs.

The other day a dear friend of mine expressed confusion over a particular aspect of this increased noise. "These are people I know," she said, "and they are nothing like that in real life." I nodded in understanding. Why would someone who is normally kind suddenly become so unmerciful online?

Then this morning I came across these words from Scripture: "Those who are peacemakers will plant seeds of peace and reap a harvest of righteousness" (James 3:18). I suddenly realized that we, as humans, so easily get mixed up about how *peace always needs to come first*. Sometimes there's an issue we're passionate about, something we're utterly convinced is right (and it may very well be). But then we decide that the *rightness* is what matters most, even more than relationships. Rather than planting seeds of peace, we sacrifice peace for the sake of declaring our position or opinion on a particular subject. We somehow feel doing so is our duty.

We probably all know someone like this—the brother-in-law who argues about politics while passing the mashed potatoes at Thanksgiving dinner, the preacher who pounds the pulpit with closed fists, the well-meaning friend who unknowingly offends the very people she wants to reach. They all have one thing in common: no matter how loud they may shout, no one is really going to listen. And if no one is listening, there is no opportunity for a response. And if there is no opportunity for a response, there is no transformation (which is true righteousness, the kind that comes from the inside out).

What's the alternative? For us to be peacemakers who love others so well that they want to hear what we have to say. To be people who value those who are different from us even if we don't understand them. To build relationships one tiny seed at a time until something strong and beautiful grows.

I believe gentleness is one of the most undervalued qualities in our culture. Yet we are invited to be "gentle at all times" (James 3:17). All times means at home, at work, in church, and on social media. Gentleness is the soil where peace can grow.

Maybe you're not the shouting kind to begin with and you've wondered if you've been too quiet in a world where everyone seems to be holding a megaphone. If so, let me encourage you to continue being gentle, continue being a peacemaker, continue planting those seeds.

Maybe you've gotten mixed up and unintentionally put being right before relationships. If so, I imagine you're weary and perhaps wounded. It's time to rest. It's time to return to peace, within your own heart and with those around you.

One of my favorite stories in all of Scripture is when God reveals himself to the prophet Elijah on a mountain. There is a mighty windstorm, an earthquake, then a fire, but God is in none of these. This line still takes my breath away: "After the fire there was a voice, a soft whisper" (1 Kings 19:12 CSB). God was in the gentleness. God was in the peace. God was in the whisper. God is *still* in the whisper. He doesn't need to turn up the volume to make himself heard. He doesn't need us to either.

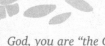

God, you are "the God of peace" (Heb. 13:20). Give me the courage to be a person of peace too. When I'm tempted to focus on making sure I'm telling everyone what's

right, help me remember what matters most is that they know how much they're loved by you. You are the One who transforms hearts gently, fully, and miraculously—including my own. Amen.

What does it mean to you to be a peacemaker?

_____

_____

_____

WE WERE MADE FROM DUST, a bit of earth kissed by heaven, and we are made to be ground breakers and peacemakers and freedom shakers.

ANN VOSKAMP

33

no punishment

Such love has no fear, because perfect love expels all fear. If we are afraid, it is for fear of punishment, and this shows that we have not fully experienced his perfect love.

1 John 4:18

She sits on the couch in my counseling office and pulls at a stray thread as she talks. She tells me how life has been hard lately. She recently lost her job. The doctor found a suspicious lump. A few days ago, a car backed into hers in the parking lot of a grocery store, denting her bumper and her hope. She looks at me and asks a simple yet complicated question: "What am I doing wrong?"

I nod in understanding, because it's not the first time I've heard this inquiry. I asked the same question at times during our journey through infertility. When life goes sideways, we want to find an explanation—and the closest one at hand is, "It must be me." But that's a lie, a stress-causer, and a peace-stealer.

Jesus said, "Here on earth you will have many trials and sorrows" (John 16:33). Why? *Because all is not as it should be.* We live suspended between Eden and eternity. All is not yet well.

The enemy of our hearts would love for us to believe that when "bad" things happen, we're being punished.

> But [Jesus] was pierced for our transgressions,
>> he was crushed for our iniquities;
> the punishment that brought us peace was on him,
>> and by his wounds we are healed. (Isa. 53:5 NIV)

Part of the miracle of the gospel is that Jesus took our punishment for us.

It matters that we know this, because otherwise we're tempted to see God as a slightly menacing figure with a lightning bolt in his hand, ready to throw it our way as soon as we do wrong. John said, "If we are afraid, it is for fear of punishment, and this shows that we have not fully experienced his perfect love" (1 John 4:18). Paul declared, "How much more shall we be saved from God's wrath through him!" (Rom. 5:9 NIV).

Yes, we experience God's discipline, but discipline is different from punishment. Discipline comes from a place of love, not anger. As in parenting, it means letting someone experience the consequence of their action. If someone shows up to work high on drugs, then he'll lose his job. If someone yells at her spouse, then distance will grow in that relationship. That's not punishment; it's experiencing the natural consequence of a choice.

Sometimes, because we live in a fallen, broken world, we're also impacted by other people's actions. The drunk driver runs the red light. The chemicals leak from the factory and contaminate our water. The economy falters, leading to layoffs. This doesn't mean we've done something wrong; it means all has not yet been made right.

Thinking about all that can go wrong in this world makes me want to find a safe place to hide. You too? If so, there's good news. The love of God is the safe haven we can run to when life gets hard.

That's why it matters so much that we don't believe he's punishing us. If we do, we'll distance ourselves when we need him most. The state of the world, the brokenness of our lives, the reality of death, and the losses we endure grieve God's heart too. He is in our hard times *with* us. He is forever *for* us. We serve a God not of lightning bolts but of love, not of meanness but of mercy, not of punishment but of peace.

God, thank you that I don't have to fear punishment because of what Jesus did on the cross. When hard things happen in my life, help me not to ask, "What am I doing wrong?" but instead remember what Jesus has done for me. You love me, you're for me, and you will make all things right in the end. Amen.

If you ever ask, "What am I doing wrong?" pause to remember what Jesus has done for you instead.

_____

_____

_____

I TRULY BELIEVE God can make beautiful things out of the broken, messed up stuff of life.

LISA LEONARD

34

a case for grace

God, have mercy on me, a sinner.

Luke 18:13 NIV

I've been to court only once, and it was stressful. Lean in close, and I'll tell you the story. In college, I had a bit of what they'd call a "lead foot." Coming home late one night on an almost-empty interstate, I watched the numbers on my speedometer climb. Seventy . . . eighty . . . eighty-nine. (I've not told this to many people, so consider yourself in the inner circle now.) Lights flashed behind me, and I knew I'd been caught. A stern but slightly amused officer handed me a ticket. A few weeks later, I appeared in court.

As I waited for my turn in front of the judge, I determined I could never be a lawyer. I'm bad at arguing and hate conflict. Yet as I've already shared, some days it feels like there's a courtroom inside of me. An inner voice puts me on trial over and over again for what I did or didn't do. I used to debate with this prosecutor. I'd justify and explain, give evidence of good behavior, call witnesses to the stand. But no matter how hard I tried, it seemed the verdict came out the same: "Guilty, guilty, guilty. Peace confiscated. Sentenced to shame."

I told my mom about my old speeding tendency at a recent family get-together. She looked suitably alarmed for a second and then laughed, knowing the current version of myself is unlikely to go roaring down the highway like a NASCAR driver. "What happened with the ticket?" she asked. "Well," I said, "I didn't fight the charge. So the court went easy on me." I did have to pay a fine and got put on probation, but my offense didn't end up permanently on my record.

I wish I'd learned more from that event than just to slow down. Because when inner charges are pressed against me, all my arguments seem to fall short. These days I've started to pray two simple prayers that are my only defense. First, "God, have mercy on me, a sinner" (Luke 18:13 NIV). This prayer was uttered by a tax collector while a Pharisee stood by praying in a way that made a case for himself, including his good deeds and how he was better than others. Jesus said the tax collector rather than the Pharisee "went home justified before God" (Luke 18:14 NIV). The other prayer I've come to love is simply declaring, "Jesus is Lord, I am loved, that is all."

There's no case the enemy of my heart can make against those truths. Yes, I *am* a sinner. But I'm also forgiven, transformed, redeemed, and a new creation. My true identity is not in my mistakes but in what God speaks over me. What Jesus has done on my behalf is irrefutable, his love for me unchangeable.

This doesn't mean I just do whatever I want. I stopped my speeding habit after that little court visit. And repentance from the heart is an essential part of our faith. But we don't have to live in condemnation. We don't have to defend ourselves. "If anybody does sin, we have an advocate with the Father—Jesus Christ, the Righteous One. He is the atoning sacrifice for our sins" (1 John 2:1–2 NIV).

Our lives are a paradox. We're guilty and entirely covered by grace. We're accused by the enemy and affirmed by our Father. We're lawbreakers made wholly righteous by what Jesus did for us. We're speeders with sneaky hearts and lead feet. But we're also saints who are new creations, beloved beyond all we can imagine.

God, thank you for your grace that is stronger than any accusation the enemy of my heart may try to bring against me. I don't have to defend myself, because you defend me. I am a sinner. Have mercy on me. You are Lord, I am loved, that is all. Amen.

Which of the two prayers in today's reading speaks most to you? Or is there another short prayer you can write here to remember when you hear inner accusations?

_____

_____

TIME STOOD STILL AS A SELF-CONDEMNING, toxic internal dialog began. Shame began to fill my heart, but as it did the Spirit of God within me gently nudged—reminding me that condemnation is not from Him. His conviction, however, spurred me on toward choosing a more godly response. I whispered a quick prayer. And as I moved in the way of grace the Lord changed the tone of my heart.

GWEN SMITH

35

having peace about it

> When you go through deep waters,
>   I will be with you.
> When you go through rivers of difficulty,
>   you will not drown.
> When you walk through the fire of oppression,
>   you will not be burned up;
>   the flames will not consume you.
>
> Isaiah 43:2

It's raining outside. Fat, sloppy drops like tears slide down the window of my office. I'm safely seated in front of my computer screen, about to do a video interview. Occasionally, thunder roars in the distance, and I'm thankful for the walls and ceiling above me. During the interview, those listening in can ask questions. It seems this group is particularly curious about how to know if we're to move forward in a dream, desire, or decision. One person offers, "Well, I need to have peace about it."

I've heard this phrase many times, and I understand the good intentions behind it. We want to be sure we're doing what's right and following God's will. Since he's a God of peace, wouldn't it make sense that we would have peace if we're doing what he wants? I've come to have a surprising, perhaps even scandalous, answer to this question: *maybe*.

If by peace we mean feeling safe and comfortable, being fairly certain that all will go well, and not fighting off fear like a pack of chihuahuas, then, no, I don't think peace is a good indication of what we're to do. If, however, we are terrified and half-crazed, uncertain and a bit insecure, and have thrown our comfort out the window in the name of obedience but inside have a deep, sustaining peace, then, yes, I think peace is a faithful barometer.

I can think of many times when a biblical character didn't have any human peace in a situation. When Jesus was in the garden of Gethsemane, he felt deep distress and prayed. "Father, if you are willing, please take this cup of suffering away from me. Yet I want your will to be done, not mine" (Luke 22:42). When God called Moses to lead the people of Israel out of Egypt, Moses had anything but peace. Moses sputtered and protested. He asked God to send someone else. Instant and outward peace was not part of the process. When God asked Jonah to go as a prophet to the city of Nineveh, Jonah had so little peace about it that he hopped on a ship to escape and ended up in the belly of a whale for three days.

Imagine if Jesus had said, "I don't have peace about going to the cross, so I'm not going to do it." History, and our story, would be very different. Emotional peace and spiritual peace are not the same.

Emotional peace says, "You'll be fine."

Spiritual peace says, "No matter what happens, God will see you through it."

Emotional peace says, "You don't have anything to be afraid of."

Spiritual peace says, "Yes, there is much to fear, but God will make you brave."

Emotional peace says, "This will be convenient and easy."

Spiritual peace says, "This will be inconvenient and hard, but nothing is impossible with God."

Emotional peace says, "Quit when it gets to be too much."

Spiritual peace says, "Persevere because God has promised you victory in the end."

I've actually found that fear and discomfort can be more of an indicator that I am to do something than a reason to walk away from it. If the human part of me is asking, "Are you out of your mind?" but the Spirit inside me is saying, "Trust me anyway," then it's likely a holy prompting.

Yes, God does want us to use wisdom and discernment, to look into his Word and get wise counsel, to consider all the options and the costs. But at the end of the day, we don't have to rely on what we feel to know what we are to do.

Instead of saying, "I have peace *about* it," perhaps we can say, "I have peace *within* me." We can have this wild, inexplicable peace even when the storm is raging, even when the future is unsure, even when our knees are knocking and our hearts are pounding. It is peace that is beyond our humanity. It is peace only the God of eternity can give.

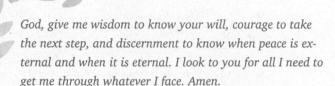

God, give me wisdom to know your will, courage to take the next step, and discernment to know when peace is external and when it is eternal. I look to you for all I need to get me through whatever I face. Amen.

How would you describe the differences between human peace and supernatural peace, which only God can give?

_____

_____

_____

TRUE PEACE IS GOD'S PEACE and can only be found in him. God's peace is not the absence of conflicts, trials or difficulties and has nothing to do with human beings or human circumstances. In fact, the true peace of God cannot be produced on a human level at all.

MARY SOUTHERLAND

36

selah for your soul

Meditate within your heart on your bed, and be still. Selah

Psalm 4:4 NKJV

I open my eyes to a new day. Instead of getting out of bed, I pull the covers up to my chin and pray about what's to come for a few moments. *Selah*

On the drive to the coffee shop where I'll write for a few hours, I turn off the radio and sit in the silence for a moment, inviting the Spirit to guide my thoughts. *Selah*

Mark and I sit at our dinner table in front of bowls full of stew, steam rising from them and thanks coming from our lips. *Selah*

We take a walk after dinner and pause to watch the cows on the other side of the fence as they turn homeward for the evening, an awkward parade that reminds me God must have a sense of humor. *Selah*

In bed again, the sun long gone behind the clouds, I think back over the day—the good, the bad, the ugly. I release it all into the hands of God like a child blowing the seeds of a dandelion into the wind. *Selah*

The word *Selah* appears over seventy times in the book of Psalms, and yet in many ways it remains a mystery. Some translations of Scripture leave it out because there is no English equivalent. Author and worship pastor Jason Soroski says, "Many commentators think that Selah meant 'to pause' or 'to reflect.' This could have been a request for the reader or listener to pause and think about what has just been said, or it could have been a space for voices to pause and for instruments to play alone. We don't really know for certain."[1]

What I do know for certain is that I need moments of Selah in my life. There have been many days unlike the one I described above—when I jumped out of bed and rushed into the day, listened to the news in the car and despaired about the state of the world, shoveled in food between tasks or meetings, ignored the cows because the chaos within me was just too loud for delight to find its way in, and fell into bed so weary I didn't have a thought left except how exhausted I was. I used to believe "busy" was a badge of honor, that it proved I had worth and was wanted. I saw anything like Selah as an interruption. But after ending up on the brink of burnout, I began to see it as an invitation.

Our God didn't design us for productivity. We need eight hours of sleep a night. Three meals a day. We're far slower than cheetahs. Less industrious than ants. We so easily forget this and think we're on this earth to do as much as we can as quickly as we can. But the God who spoke the world into being in six days has no trouble with his to-do list.

What if the pauses in our lives are more important than what we can produce? To be honest, this question scares me. To come to God simply as I am with nothing in my hands seems to be an act of great vulnerability. But this is exactly why I need Selah. Because without pausing, I forget how much I'm loved. I forget that I have nothing to prove. I forget that I'm made not for striving but for relationship. Selah is the opposite of stress.

Selah is placed with intention throughout the Psalms. We can also place it intentionally throughout our days. It's tempting to think we need to wait until we go on vacation or even retire to slow down. But Selah tells us the peace of God can be found in the here and now, wherever we are. Selah goes well with morning coffee and the cozy corner of a couch, with prayer closets and carpool lines. Anywhere we can find a sliver of time. Selah doesn't demand hours. It asks only for a deep breath, a few moments, a pause in the middle of the rush. How those little bits of time can make a big difference in our lives is much like the meaning of Selah itself—a mystery but deeply true just the same.

God, you invite me not to productivity but to intimacy. When I'm tempted to hurry through my days, draw me back to your heart. Show me how to choose peace in not only big ways but also small, everyday ones. Amen.

What's a recent moment when you experienced Selah?

_____

_____

_____

SLOWING DOWN GIVES GOD A CHANCE to deal with my chaos in my house and in my heart so I can really see how He loves me.

SUZIE LIND

37

who God is

The Son is the radiance of God's glory and the exact representation of his being.

Hebrews 1:3 NIV

Neal Caffrey makes me want to be a thief and a liar. Yep. He's the main character on a show called *White Collar*. Neal, finally caught for crimes like fraud and forgery, is released to the care of the FBI in return for helping them with cases. He has many talents, but the one that makes me want to be him (perhaps just for a day) is his ability to replicate works of art perfectly.

I, however, struggle to draw stick figures. When I speak, I go through a process where I write out much of what I want to say, pare that down to an outline, and as a final step, draw the main points. Mark finds this amusing and calls these doodles "hieroglyphics." He'll point to something on my little notecard and say, "Is that a cat?" to which I will reply indignantly, "No, that's Moses and the burning bush." Because of my lack of artistic ability, I'm in awe of anyone who has such a skill—even if they are a white-collar criminal recruited by the FBI.

Thanks to Neal Caffrey, I know a replica must be precise to the point that even experts can't tell the difference. If it's a painting, not even a brushstroke can vary. If it's a sculpture, every line and curve must be repeated. The author of Hebrews tells us that Jesus is the "exact representation" of God, and the original meaning of this phrase is "replica." This truth about God's nature seems obvious as I'm typing it, but when I read it in Hebrews, I realized I had thought there were some subtle differences between Son and Father. Sometimes I believed . . .

Jesus is always compassionate. God is impatient.

Jesus is always with me. God can be distant.

Jesus is always accepting of my humanity. God is exasperated by my imperfections.

If you had given me a "true or false" quiz on the characteristics of God, *of course* I would have marked every statement I just made about him as false. Such beliefs often live just beyond the edge of our awareness, buried under old hurts or bad information. But they matter because they affect us—they infect us—in powerful ways.

One of the peace-stealers in my life has been the idea that God and Jesus are somehow playing "good cop/bad cop" with me. That God is the one I have to watch out for, while Jesus is full of mercy. God sometimes seemed mysterious to the point of being unknowable. I figured I would find out more about him when I got to heaven. But to see who God is, I only need to look at who Jesus was when he was on this earth. "So Jesus explained, 'I tell you the truth, the Son can do nothing by himself. He does only what he sees the Father doing. Whatever the Father does, the Son also does. For the Father loves the Son and shows him everything he is doing'" (John 5:19–20).

The compassion of Jesus is the compassion of God.

The gentleness of Jesus is the gentleness of God.

The love of Jesus is the love of God.

When God sent his Son to earth, he sent not just a *representation* but also a *replica*. Every brushstroke the same. Every line and curve repeated. God took all of his grandness and mystery, wrapped it in skin, laid it in a manger, walked it through the dusty streets of Jerusalem, hung it from a cross, and raised it from a tomb. He took the eternal and invisible and made it earthly and tangible.

This is the miracle, the truth that's beyond forgery: all of who God is dwelled in Jesus, who dwelled with us, who now dwells in me.

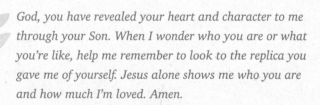

God, you have revealed your heart and character to me through your Son. When I wonder who you are or what you're like, help me remember to look to the replica you gave me of yourself. Jesus alone shows me who you are and how much I'm loved. Amen.

I was unaware of how I sometimes saw God and Jesus differently until I read Hebrews 1:3 and paused to think about it. Take a moment to do the same, and see if you might have unintentionally done this too. Write down anything you discover.

_____

_____

_____

HERE'S WHAT I KNOW ABOUT GOD: He has not left your side. He is there, walking right beside you. . . . Because He loves you.

SHELLY WILDMAN

38

just be faithful

The master was full of praise. "Well done, my good and faithful servant. You have been faithful in handling this small amount, so now I will give you many more responsibilities. Let's celebrate together!"

Matthew 25:21

Despite my best intentions, I still eat vanilla ice cream right out of the carton. I sometimes wrestle anxiety like a wild alligator. I feel confused by social media and stressed out by the news. Curled up in bed, I tell all this to Jesus one day. And I ask, "What do you want me to picture as success?" It seems the answer that comes quietly into the dark is this: *faithfulness*.

This is not the answer our world would give. We'd be told fame or material possessions, staying young forever or getting to sit at the cool table are markers of success. But in the Gospels, the master doesn't say, "Well done, my good and famous servant." He says, "Well done, my good and *faithful* servant" (Matt. 25:21, emphasis mine).

This morning I read an endearingly human story about the disciples. Jesus has been crucified. Their lives are in turmoil. They're unsure of what the future holds. Peter says, "I'm going fishing" (John 21:3). Haven't we all had those days? We throw up our hands and say, "I'm going to get a latte," "I'm going shopping," or "I'm going to the gym." We turn to what we know. The disciples fish all night and catch nothing. Then Jesus appears, although they don't yet know it's him, and he tells them to let out their nets one more time. They catch so many fish, they can hardly handle them all.

This is faithfulness. It's continuing to cast the net because Jesus says so. Even when we've been up all night. Even when we're weary. Even when we're confused. Even when we're discouraged and want to quit. Our role is obedience; God's role is results.

Eugene Peterson describes faithfulness as "a long obedience in the same direction."[1] It's not sexy. It doesn't make headlines. We're not likely to get awards, applause, or even an abundance of "likes" for it. But faithfulness is quietly, often invisibly, life altering and world changing.

I want to be faithful to Jesus for a lifetime.

I want to be faithful to use my gift of writing for a lifetime.

I want to be faithful to my husband for a lifetime.

I want to be faithful to intentionally cultivate friendships with other women for a lifetime.

I used to think that what mattered most was growth. The difficulty with that is we can't control growth. God alone is the

One who makes things grow (see 1 Cor. 3:6–7). We are instead invited to be faithful, to plant and water. Out of that naturally comes growth, but we don't make it happen. That feels like a weight off our shoulders. One of the keys to peace is not taking on what God has never asked us to carry.

If you're putting pressure on yourself today to do more, be more, achieve more, then pause and take a deep breath. *Just be faithful.* If you're comparing yourself to others in life or ministry and feel you're falling short, refocus on your own journey. *Just be faithful.* If you're striving for perfection and trying to make everyone happy, let go of those unrealistic demands. *Just be faithful.*

We don't need big resolutions. We don't need to check every item off our bucket list. We don't have to prove our worth. Instead, we can simply say, "Jesus, I will do what I can, where I am, in this moment to love you and others today. Then I will do it again tomorrow."

That's faithfulness.

That's powerful.

That's enough for a lifetime.

God, thank you that you invite me into faithfulness. You're a God not of pressure but peace, not of heaviness but hope, not of relentless striving but relationship. I ask for the

courage and wisdom to simply do what I can, where I am, with what I have to love you and others today. Amen.

What's one small way you can love Jesus and others where you are, as you are, with what you have today?

_____

_____

_____

A FAITHFUL LIFE USUALLY DOESN'T RECEIVE a lot of accolades. Faithful people tend to get overlooked, since they are about the little things, not the big ones. . . . And therein lies the faith of faithfulness. It is believing in the unseen and trusting that this humble life is the best life, because it is the one He asks of you.

JOY DOMBROW

39

go and show

As he entered a village there, ten men with leprosy stood at a dis-
tance, crying out, "Jesus, Master, have mercy on us!" He looked at
them and said, "Go show yourselves to the priests." And as they
went, they were cleansed of their leprosy.

Luke 17:12–14

I'm sitting in front of a phone waiting for it to ring. I haven't done
this since junior high when I hoped the cute boy in science class
would call me on the supercool black-and-white phone I got for
my thirteenth birthday. I feel just as much angst in this moment.

Then it happens—the phone lights up, so I press a purple button
and say, "Thank you for calling KLRC. This is Holley. How can I pray
for you?" I'm volunteering at our local radio station taking prayer
requests for two hours. It's the kickoff to the week of Shareathon,
when KLRC receives most of the donations it needs for the year.

But nothing is being asked of the people on the other end of
the line except for them to share their hearts and stories, which

they do. I say "Amen" about half a dozen times before one of the hosts approaches me between calls, holding a microphone in his hand. "Holley," he says, "what would you say to the folks listening right now who are struggling with fear and anxiety?"

Then I say, right on the airwaves going out to over one hundred thousand people in my town and many others around the internet, "I've personally struggled with fear and anxiety for most of my life. If you're fighting those battles too, it doesn't mean you're weak; it means you're a warrior."

I say this without hesitation, although years ago it wouldn't have been so easy. I no longer feel shame about my struggles, and I've learned this secret: Every time I speak them out loud, they lose a little more of their power. I become a little more healed. I gain a little more peace.

I think of the story of the ten lepers. "Jesus, Master, have mercy on us!" they cried (Luke 17:13). His answer? "Go show yourselves to the priests" (v. 14).

It's what happens next that amazes me. "And *as they went*, they were cleansed" (v. 14, emphasis added). It's tempting to hold back and stay stuck because we think we have to be completely healed before we *go and show*. We want our story to already have the happy ending, the bow to be tied around the package, the scars to be faded into invisibility. But I've found, as the lepers did, that the healing often happens along the way.

After my words air on the radio, the phones ring again. My friend, who's sitting next to me, hands me her headset and says, "She's asking for you." I listen to a woman as she shares her still-in-progress story. I can almost see her rising up from the ground, placing her feet on the dusty road, and taking the next step in the direction Jesus has asked her to go by faith.

You don't have to wait for your healing to be complete before you start moving forward. You don't have to be whole before God sends you out. Of course we want healing to be a onetime, instantaneous event. We can even feel guilty if it's not. But I've found healing is more often a process. Sometimes when we ask God to move, he's asking us the same.

Nothing has the power to hold you back.

You are already worthy.

And God is already at work.

God, thank you that I don't have to be perfect to be part of your plan. You aren't asking me to hold back until my healing is complete. Instead, you invite me to obey today. You give me a path to follow. You are transforming my life with every step. Amen.

How has God healed you, whether emotionally, physically, or spiritually?

_____

_____

GOD SENT HIS SON to make sure that all of our stories, even the hard ones, are used for His glory.

BRITTA ELLIS LAFONT

40

a new perspective

Humans do not see what the LORD sees, for humans see what is visible, but the LORD sees the heart.

1 Samuel 16:7 CSB

I'm leaning against a red door in an alley that has gravel with bits of green grass growing through it. When I look up, I can see blue sky and a small window where a man in an orange shirt is working at a computer. He waves. I wave back. Then I try to focus on the commands I'm being given. "Drop your shoulder. Tilt your head. Stick your hip out."

My photographer is eight months pregnant. Occasionally, she pauses to catch her breath. Then she starts snapping pictures again. My two friends, also part of this photo shoot, tell me jokes from the sidelines in an attempt to make my smile genuine. But there's really no need—I'm having fun. Every year or so I need new pictures to use on my books and my site. Getting them taken can feel like a chore, but not today.

When the photographer is done, she declares, "Perfect!" and I find myself wishing she could stand next to me in front of my mirror each morning to offer the same affirmation. I realize that what she sees is not the same as what I do. She's a beauty hunter with a gift for finding and capturing what's lovely. When she looks at me, she's not focused on my flaws. She's looking for my best features, the lighting that will make the most of them, and how to convey not only my face but also my heart.

Because of this, I relaxed in front of her camera. The bit of nervousness I'd felt on the way over dissipated. As I stood there, I wondered why this would be so. I realized that when we can see ourselves, or our circumstances, from a different perspective, it often helps bring us peace.

There's a fancy psychological word for this: *reframing*. Counselors and authors Linda and Charlie Bloom explain, "When we change our point of view on any given situation, the facts remain the same, but a deliberate shift is made in how we see it."[1] Reframing has been shown to contribute to better mental health, decreased anxiety, and increased resilience.

As believers, we have a powerful way of reframing: we can choose to see ourselves and our circumstances from God's perspective.

We see ourselves as broken. He sees us as beloved.

We see our circumstances as impossible. He sees a bigger plan.

We see our sin. He sees what Jesus did for us on the cross.

We see what's temporary. He sees what's eternal.

We see our limits. He sees how we can do anything through him.

When we find ourselves struggling with our thoughts, we can pause and ask, "God, how do you see me right now? How do you see my circumstances?"

We may worry that God's view of us is harsh or judgmental, but "there is no condemnation for those who belong to Christ Jesus" (Rom. 8:1). Because of what Jesus did for us, God looks at us with love and grace. He is relentlessly *for* us. He is not looking for our flaws; he's looking for our best features—the ones he created, the ones he wants to use for a purpose. He's also looking at our best future, the one beyond our current situation and concerns that he's working out even now.

Before we part ways, I hug my photographer and say, "Thank you." As I walk down the street back to my car, I feel a little less self-conscious than when I arrived, a little more comfortable in my own skin.

I thought I needed new pictures. What I needed even more was a new perspective.

God, you are the only One who can see it all—past, present, and future. You also see so much deeper than the surface. You see what's eternally true. I want to see myself and my circumstances through your eyes today. Realign my view with yours. Bring me peace through a new perspective. Amen.

Pause and ask, "God, how do you see me right now? How do you see my circumstances?"

_____

_____

_____

BECAUSE WE SEE THE WORLD FROM OUR OWN, individual points of view, our perspectives are unique. Sometimes sharing that perspective is a gift to someone who doesn't see what you see.

DAWN CAMP

41

when life gets hard

Now if we are children, then we are heirs—heirs of God and co-heirs with Christ, if indeed we share in his sufferings in order that we may also share in his glory.

Romans 8:17 NIV

Sara Frankl spent the last years of her life confined within the walls of her home due to a debilitating medical condition. Still a young woman, she had to face that many of her God-sized dreams—like marrying and raising a family—would not come true the way she'd imagined. And yet she held tight to the dream that mattered most to her: encouraging others with her words. She could no longer do that at an office job, but she continued to do so from her laptop at home. After Sara slipped home to Jesus, hundreds of stories of lives she had quietly and privately changed came pouring out on the internet.

I don't know what Sara imagined her life would be like when she grew up, but I'm certain the illness she faced was not part of the plan. She could have given up or given in to self-pity. Instead, she persevered and chose to see her limitations as opportunities.

In *How People Grow*, Henry Cloud and John Townsend say,

> Jesus turns our natural bents upside down. In the world's view, the path to glory is being "on top of it" or "having it all together." In Jesus' way, the path to glory is experiencing pain and suffering: "Now if we are children, then we are heirs—heirs of God and co-heirs with Christ, if indeed we share in his sufferings in order that we may also share in his glory" (Rom. 8:17).[1]

When we think of God's will for our lives, it's easy to picture a path that takes us away from suffering rather than into it. Yet Scripture shows us again and again that suffering is part of the journey. That means when life gets hard, we don't have to say, "I must be doing something wrong." Instead, we can find comfort in knowing that Christ himself faced suffering as he fulfilled his mission of redeeming the world.

This comes with a caveat: we are talking about *purposeful* suffering. Cloud and Townsend add, "He chose the path of the cross because of the fruit it would bear for all of us. Yet he refused to enter suffering that would be inappropriate for his purposes."[2] In other words, suffering for the sake of suffering is not what God has in mind. Sometimes we go to the other extreme and believe we must suffer all the time in order to be godly. But Scripture makes it clear that God desires a life of joy for us. Suffering is intended to be temporary—whether it is resolved in this life or when we enter eternity. God wants us to thrive. Even Jesus endured the cross "for the joy set before him" (Heb. 12:2 NIV). So we are not to be surprised by suffering, yet we're also not to simply accept it as the way things must be forever. We can ask God, "What is your purpose in this?"

You will have hard days. You will face disappointments. You will experience setbacks. Yet, in the middle of this, you can trust that God's purposes will prevail and you are truly, deeply loved. That enables you to do what Sara did—choose joy and let nothing stand in the way of completing God's purpose for your life.

God, thank you that I can trust you even in the middle of suffering. Jesus knows what it's like to experience pain on the path to a greater purpose, and that's comforting to me. I ask that you give me the strength, courage, and hope I need to move forward no matter what happens in my life. Amen.

Who in your life is going through a difficult time? Send a card, make a phone call, or find another way to share words of encouragement with that person today.

_____

_____

_____

_____

HE KNOWS MY PAST, PRESENT, AND FUTURE. He is surprised by nothing. He is with me, never leaves me even when I feel alone, and holds me up even when I think I am standing on my own two feet. He is good. All the time.

SARA FRANKL

42

peace on earth

Glory to God in the highest,
And on earth peace, goodwill toward men!

Luke 2:14 NKJV

We've read the story and know the scene. The unshowered shepherds with the wide-eyed flock around them. The shock then awe. The angels indescribable, declaring the good news. The star and the manger. The baby and the hope.

Yes, I've read the story, yet this time one phrase keeps echoing in my heart: "Peace, goodwill toward men." It seems peace and goodwill have sometimes been missing lately in our world. They've gotten lost somewhere in the angry social media posts. The sides taken and the lines drawn. The fists raised and the shouts heard.

When I see the phrase "peace, goodwill toward men," I feel a little homesick. The way we do when we have to spend Christmas far away in a place we weren't ever intended to, where we really don't belong. Because we are made for love. For grace. For understanding. For togetherness. For joy.

There's a lot God could have chosen to say that night. He could have dealt with politics (which had its troubles then too). He could have made moral proclamations. He could have taken a tone like a ruler-tapping teacher and told us all to get our acts together. But, instead, he blessed us. He spoke words of encouragement and hope.

What if the whole world did the same? What if we all put down our opinions and picked up grace? Shut our mouths and opened our doors. Pulled back our judgments and reached out our hands. Banished our angry words and brought out the welcome mat for kindness and mercy.

It's scary, I know. Because it might seem as if everything will go wrong if we dare to make ourselves vulnerable.

But if that's what God chose to do, can't we?

Sometimes we forget that Someone already came to save the world. That job has been taken. That task marked complete. It is not on our shoulders. And this is what Jesus told us will continue that mission: "A new command I give you: Love one another" (John 13:34 NIV).

Peace on earth, goodwill toward men.

It's the good news of the gospel. It's what we need so much more than one more angry Facebook post. More than another television tirade. More than fists and voices raised. And this good news hasn't changed. So, Dear World, could it be time that we do?

Let's make this day all about love. All about peace, goodwill toward men. Which is really just another way of saying let's make it all about Jesus.

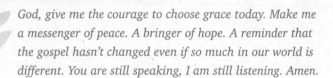

God, give me the courage to choose grace today. Make me a messenger of peace. A bringer of hope. A reminder that the gospel hasn't changed even if so much in our world is different. You are still speaking, I am still listening. Amen.

What's a situation in which you're tempted to speak harsh words instead of peaceful ones? What could you say instead today?

_____

_____

_____

THEN PEALED THE BELLS MORE LOUD AND DEEP:
"God is not dead, nor doth He sleep;
    The Wrong shall fail,
    The Right prevail,
With peace on earth, good-will to men."

HENRY WADSWORTH LONGFELLOW

43

less worry, more worship

For the Lord GOD, the Holy One of Israel, has said:
"You will be delivered by returning and resting;
your strength will lie in quiet confidence.
But you are not willing."

Isaiah 30:15 CSB

"I'm stressed out," I confessed to friends over lunch one day. "What's going on?" they asked. I shrugged and said, "I don't really know." They hugged me and promised to pray.

That night I pulled out my art journal, plugged headphones into my ears, and grabbed a Sharpie. I wanted to think through my life—and especially my work. I began to put "Writer" at the top of the page because that's my title. But as I leaned toward the paper, I felt a bit of hesitation and silently asked God, "What do you want me to write in that spot?" And it seemed I heard one word in response: worshiper.

And suddenly I knew why I was so exhausted. *I'd switched from being a worshiper to being a worker.* This isn't the first time it's happened. Throughout my life when I've felt pressure mount-ing and expectations building, I've tended to have one response: try harder. It's a heart reflex I've had since high school. Be more. Do more. Go more. I carry on like that until I get worn out and a bit rebellious.

Yes, I should have caught on a bit quicker to that pattern by now. But I'm somewhat of a slow learner in this area, it seems. Maybe you have one of those areas in your life too? Thankfully, we serve a God of grace. A God who chases us down right in the middle of all our wild and weary-making running. A God who speaks life and peace and rest into us. A God who wants our hearts more than our hands.

I spelled out the letters slowly: w-o-r-s-h-i-p-e-r. And I thought of this verse:

> Better to have one handful with quietness
> than two handfuls with hard work
> and chasing the wind. (Eccles. 4:6)

I sensed God asking me, "Can you be satisfied with one handful?" Because here's how we're meant to live: with one hand holding tight to what God has given us—love, joy, peace, grace, goodness. And the other hand empty and open for whatever else he would have us receive. Two handfuls means we're clenching our fists through life. We're gritting our teeth. We're hanging on with all our might. Two handfuls means we're tired.

Thankfully, God generously offers us what all tired people need—*rest*. Even if the world around us keeps unavoidably spinning—the toddlers keep throwing Cheerios, the projects keep coming, the calendar keeps filling—we can wrap our fingers around peace in a way that truly does pass understanding. And we can let go of all we've grasped that was never meant for us. We can reach out and take hold of the peace that has been promised us today. And we can let go of our striving so we can receive what's infinitely better: God's unconditional love and grace.

I filled the page in my art journal with words and prayers. Then I laid down my pen. And when I also laid down my head on the pillow that night, I felt different. Not so weary and afraid. Quieter inside. More like a worshiper, less like a worker.

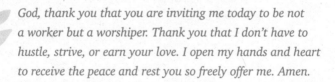

God, thank you that you are inviting me today to be not a worker but a worshiper. Thank you that I don't have to hustle, strive, or earn your love. I open my hands and heart to receive the peace and rest you so freely offer me. Amen.

If you're tempted to wear yourself out, what's driving you? What truth can help you rest?

_____

_____

_____

_____

GOD HAS EVERYTHING IN HIS HANDS ALREADY, and sometimes I just need a time-out for a few moments to remind myself that God's got everything under control.

He delivers us when we return to Him, when we rest in Him. Every time.

DENISE HUGHES

44

different and the same

For I am about to do something new.
See, I have already begun!
Isaiah 43:19

Jesus Christ is the same yesterday, today, and forever.
Hebrews 13:8

The sun is a debutante this morning, wearing a dress of crimson and gold laced with clouds. I stand on the beach, snap photos, then post, "Have you ever fallen in love with a place? It's been over a decade since I first visited Hilton Head, and it still makes me swoon." I love the salty air, tall seagrass, demanding seagulls, dolphins with sleek backs, dogs let off their leashes who chase yellow balls into the waves.

Most of all, I love that the ocean is two things: absolutely consistent and never the same. The tides come in and out in intervals so steady, a chart predicts them by the minute. Yet what the waves bring in is a continual surprise—starfish, sand dollars, an abundance of shells, driftwood that could tell you a long, beautiful story about all the places it's been.

I think we, as humans, crave both the familiar and the new. Too much of the first and we become bored and restless. Too much of the latter and we're anxious and uncertain. We serve a God who says, "I am about to do something new" (Isa. 43:19) and yet "is the same yesterday, today, and forever" (Heb. 13:8). This can seem like a paradox, but I understand it when I have sand beneath my feet.

God's heart, character, and ways do not vary. We can count on them not just by the hour but by the minute. But how he shows up, what he brings to us, his mercies and miracles—these are always brand-new, never repeated. Worry reverses these truths. It tempts us to believe God has changed. He is not as reliable as we'd hoped. He might not be who he says he is. We hear an echo of the enemy of our hearts from Eden who hissed, "Did God really say . . . ?" Worry tells us that things will always be the same. Our circumstances will not and cannot change.

I've carried a concern with me like a shell in my pocket, the rough edges rubbing against my heart. As I watch the sun rise, I feel ready to release it. I recall God is always good. Forever loving. He is working out his plans.

Has he ever spoken and failed to act?
  Has he ever promised and not carried it through? (Num. 23:19)

Our God is bigger than the ocean, more faithful than the waves, and at the start of each new day, we can trust him all over again.

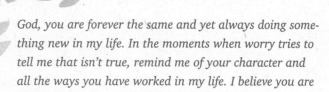

God, you are forever the same and yet always doing something new in my life. In the moments when worry tries to tell me that isn't true, remind me of your character and all the ways you have worked in my life. I believe you are good and mighty, loving and powerful. I trust you with all that concerns me today. Amen.

What's one part of God's character you're grateful is always the same? And what's one new thing you see him doing in your life?

_____

_____

_____

THE RESPONSE I GET ISN'T about my circumstances. It's always about him. My heavenly Father gently whispers to my soul . . . "I've got this. I've got you. I'm doing a new thing. Just abide in me."

ELISA PULLIAM

45

take heart

I have told you these things, so that in me you may have peace. In this world you will have trouble. But take heart! I have overcome the world.

John 16:33 NIV

I turn over in my bed, pull my favorite blanket up to my chin, and burrow deeper into my pillow. But my mind is a cranky toddler refusing to surrender to the nap she desperately needs.

Earlier in the evening, I texted a dear friend a list of my concerns. They included a loved one with a significant health problem, someone I cared about making a decision that I could only see leading to disaster, and a discouraging conversation I kept replaying in my mind. My friend offered some advice and then said, "I love that these feelings bear witness to how deeply you love and care about these people in your life. The more we love, the deeper we feel."

I hadn't thought of it that way before. It's true that I've always been empathetic and engaged. I sometimes envy people who can walk through life without seeming to be affected by what's going on around them. I'm not that kind of person. I'm disturbed by the news stories. I worry about those I love. Sometimes I can't sleep because I just want everyone and everything to be okay.

In other words, I take things to heart. This is one of my greatest strengths. It makes me a caring daughter, a kind friend, a thoughtful wife, a compassionate writer. But on days like this one, it's also one of my greatest struggles.

I decide there's only one solution: I will barricade my heart. I won't feel anything! I won't care about anyone! I will fall asleep immediately every single night.

It takes about three seconds before I realize not only is this impossible, but it's not what I really want to do. What now? In the middle of the darkness and discouragement, I have a realization: God never asked me to take everything to heart. He did tell me, "In this world you will have trouble. But take heart! I have overcome the world" (John 16:33 NIV).

When I take something to heart, I believe it's all on me.

When I take heart in Jesus, I remember he's in control.

When I take something to heart, I feel like I'm alone.

When I take heart in Jesus, I know he will never let me go.

When I take something to heart, I lose my hope.

When I take heart in Jesus, I find him at work even in the hardest circumstances.

Taking heart simply means taking whatever concerns me to Jesus. That's what I finally do as the minutes move toward midnight. At some point, I drift off to sleep.

When I wake up, it's a new morning. My challenges remain, but my perspective has changed. Whatever this day brings, I don't have to carry it on my own. I can give it to the only One strong enough to take it.

God, thank you for giving me a heart that feels deeply. That's your design, and it is good. In the moments when I'm tempted to take everything to heart, help me remember that, instead, I can take everything to you. You are still in control. You are still taking care of me. You will take care of everyone else too. Amen.

What are you taking to heart today? Pause and take it to Jesus instead.

_____

_____

IF THERE IS ONE THING I HAVE LEARNED in this journey of taking care of my heart, it's that trying to tend to it on my own without the Father's loving guidance is only a recipe for disaster. . . . I need to trust that God in all His goodness will take care of my body, mind, spirit, and heart, that He will graciously handle my hopes, dreams, and desires.

JAZMIN N. FRANK

46

anger is okay

Be angry, and do not sin.
Ephesians 4:26 NKJV

I'm sitting in a booth at a café with my *More Than Small Talk* podcast cohosts, Suzanne Eller and Jennifer Watson. We meet once a month to plan episodes, and right now we're brainstorming one titled "Gratitude When You Have an Attitude." We've already tackled depression and anxiety. I had no fear about sharing my battle with those two. But now I look at my friends and ask, "Do I really have to admit to people that I get annoyed sometimes?"

Later I keep thinking about my response. Why is it hard for me to own my anger? In their book, *Good Women Get Angry*, psychologists Gary Oliver and H. Norman Wright say anger is not only inevitable but also essential. "This was probably not the message you heard when you were growing up. If you are like many women, you probably heard, 'Don't rock the boat. Be a peacemaker. Your job is to nurture others.'"[1]

As I've tried to understand my anger, these three discoveries have helped.

- *Anger is armor.* Conflict resolution specialists say, "Anger is often called a secondary emotion because we tend to resort to anger in order to protect ourselves from or cover up other vulnerable feelings. A primary feeling is what is felt immediately before we feel anger. We almost always feel something else first before we get angry."[2] It can help to ask, "What did I feel just before I got angry?" or "What am I afraid of or trying to protect?"

- *Anger is related to our values.* A dear friend of mine has a daughter with special needs and fights hard to get her the best care possible. In a recent situation, an unfair decision based on a hospital policy kept that from happening. My friend was furious and yet kept saying, "I shouldn't feel this way." I told her, "You're mad because you value your daughter's well-being, and that is a beautiful thing." To find the source of our anger, we can ask, "What value of mine is being violated right now?"

- *Anger is informative.* During our conversation, Jennifer said, "I think for me in the past, getting angry felt like a sin. . . . My counselor said anger is just information."[3] The verse at the start of this devotion says, "Be angry, and do not sin." But Jennifer's old translation (and mine) would say, "Don't be angry, because it's a sin."

Those are two *very* different meanings. Emotions make great messengers but bad bosses. We can ask, "What is my anger telling me?" then "What action is God asking me to take?"

For most of my life, I had one response to anger: stuff it down as far as it would go. But I'm learning that if I always "keep the peace," then I will never keep my peace. Maybe your story is the opposite, and anger has been a destructive volcano in your life. Either way, Oliver and Wright say, "You are going to experience anger in your life for many reasons. And when you do, it's important that you face your anger, accept it, hear the message that it is conveying to you, and learn to express your anger in a healthy way. Your anger needs your respect and attention."[4]

When God created our human minds and hearts, he gave us anger along with all the emotions we need to process life. And when we give our anger back to him, he can use it in powerful, healing ways.

God, thank you for my emotions and how each one has a purpose. I ask that you help me understand my anger and use it in the ways you intended. When I'm afraid of anger, give me the courage not to ignore it. When anger tries to control me, give me the strength to yield only to you. Amen.

Growing up, what were you taught about anger?
Anger is . . .

_____

_____

After reading today's devotion, what's one new truth
you've learned about anger?

_____

_____

IT WAS A RELIEF TO ME TO DISCOVER that anger itself
can't be a sin because we see MANY examples in Scripture of God
angry. . . . We are called by a holy God to model His behavior
even and especially in our anger.

LISA-JO BAKER

47

stronger every day

We know that suffering produces perseverance; perseverance, character; and character, hope.

Romans 5:3–4 NIV

I set my laptop on a chair in the corner of my bedroom, close the door, pull down the blinds, and click Play. I'm about to begin a fitness video, and I want no witnesses. For the last two months, I've been part of an online exercise group. Each day we complete a different workout. Some involve weights, others resistance bands, and all of them mean I have to do tough, awkward things.

Here's the catch: I'm supposed to report back to my group every day about how I did. But no one is there when I'm working out. The instructor says things like "Don't quit! Keep going! You can do this." But she can't see me through the screen. I could get away with anything. When I started the program, I looked at the weights I would have to lift and thought they would be my biggest challenge. But I was wrong. My greatest challenge has been fighting the urge to avoid anything that feels hard.

I'm not talking about the times when doing everything in the video would lead to actual injury. Sometimes I can't complete a set of push-ups because I'm out of breath. Sometimes the instructor uses heavy weights and I use none at all. I know my body and honor its limits.

What I'm talking about here is the temptation to listen to the tiny voice in the back of my mind that whispers, "Stop the video, eat a brownie, and sit on the couch. No one will know. Nothing will happen." But that voice is a liar, because something *will* happen. Unless I choose to get stronger, over time I will become weaker.

We all have this voice in our lives. It's the one that tells us the way to handle stress is by having another drink, buying one more thing we don't need, or burying our feelings at the bottom of a gallon of ice cream. "You should never feel bad," it tells us. "You can make all the hurt go away right now."

Giving in to that voice is like refusing to do the challenging part of my workouts. Yes, in the moment it actually does feel a lot better. But in the long term I would be cheating myself. The apostle Paul said, "We know that suffering produces perseverance; perseverance, character; and character, hope" (Rom. 5:3–4 NIV). When I push through a workout, it hurts and it's hard. But next time I can do a little more for a little longer (perseverance). Over time, this actually changes my body and who I am (character). I get stronger and know I can handle more than ever before (hope).

This is the emotional process God invites us into as well. We need to lift the "weight" of life, because that's how we become resilient. Again, I'm not talking about doing so to the point of injury. I've battled depression, and I couldn't have lifted the weight on my own. I needed a counselor, a doctor, and supportive friends. In some situations, asking for help is the strongest, best thing to do. I'm talking about the normal pain and annoyances of life in an imperfect world. We can avoid them in many ways, but we can only overcome them by not taking the easy way out.

When I get to the end of the workout, I'm sweaty and exhausted. But I've done more than I thought I could. I didn't give up. I didn't walk away. I showed up and gave it my best today. And that's enough to make me stronger for tomorrow.

God, you tell us that sometimes suffering is what makes us stronger. Give me the wisdom to know when to push through the pain and when to ask for help. When I'm tempted to choose what weakens me, fill me with the power I need to persevere. I will not give up. I am getting stronger every day. Amen.

What are some situations, like exercise or a hard circumstance you've made it through, when suffering actually strengthened you?

IN OUR SUFFERING, we experience the fullness of God's grace.

JEN ROLAND

48

water-walking

Peter went over the side of the boat and walked on the water toward Jesus. But when he saw the strong wind and the waves, he was terrified and began to sink. "Save me, Lord!" he shouted. Jesus immediately reached out and grabbed him. "You have so little faith," Jesus said. "Why did you doubt me?" When they climbed back into the boat, the wind stopped.

Matthew 14:29–32

I grew up near the Texas coast, where hurricanes roar in every few years. My family and I would gather around the television and watch a drenched weather reporter clinging to a light pole while the wind whipped around him and waves crashed in the background. I never once thought, *Wow, that looks fun. I wish I could go take a walk out there right now.*

These scenes come to mind when I read the story of Peter deciding to walk on water toward Jesus. Imagine for a moment what it must have been like for Peter to step out onto the waves in pitch darkness with a storm howling around him.

In *If You Want to Walk on Water, You've Got to Get Out of the Boat*, John Ortberg says, "The water is rough. The waves are high. The wind is strong. There's a storm out there. And if you get out of the boat—whatever your boat might happen to be—there's a good chance you might sink. But if you don't get out of the boat, there's a guaranteed certainty that you will never walk on the water."[1]

When life gets difficult, we all tend to take fewer risks. During hurricanes and in many situations, that's the wisest decision. We shift our focus to preventing further loss, guarding what we value, and maintaining the status quo. But sometimes Jesus shows up at the most inconvenient, scary time and asks us to take a step of faith we never expected—especially not right now.

In those moments, we have an opportunity to walk on water, but doing so requires stepping outside of our comfort zone. Ortberg says, "Your boat is whatever represents safety and security to you apart from God himself. Your boat is whatever you are tempted to put your trust in, especially when life gets a little stormy."[2]

In the biblical story, Peter decides to take the risk. We often stop the story when Peter begins to sink and Jesus reaches out his hand to save him. But I'm fascinated by what happens next. "When they climbed back into the boat, the wind stopped" (Matt. 14:32).

One day I had a huge aha moment: Peter *did* successfully walk on water. He did so with Jesus all the way back to the boat! And when they made it, the storm subsided.

Jesus may be asking you to step out of the boat in some area of your life today. You look around and think, *Not now, Lord! Wait until things settle down!* You're not sure about walking on water in general, but if you're going to do it, you'd probably much rather have the lake be as smooth as glass and not even a breeze blowing.

But if you dare to take that step of faith despite your fear, it may be the very thing that brings you closer to Jesus, lets you experience more than you ever imagined with him, and perhaps even leads you to the moment when the storm finally subsides.

God, I thank you that you have more in store for me than I can even imagine. I sense that you are asking me to take a step of faith by _____. Please give me the courage to step out and come to you. Amen.

What's a step of faith you took in the past, and how did you see Jesus helping you?

_____

_____

_____

WHATEVER WAVES YOU ARE FACING TODAY, friend, know this: They are no match for those who are courageous to live by faith. You don't have to dwell in doubt or let fear have the final say. Look it straight in the eyes and shout, "Not today!" Press into Jesus and keep your eyes fixed on him.

The journey of faith may be full of unknowns, but with Jesus, you'll discover that though the waters rage, you will always rise above.

LAUREN GASKILL

49

the joy ahead

For the joy set before him he endured the cross.

Hebrews 12:2 NIV

I'm sitting with friends in a coffee shop. One describes a recent situation in her life that left her feeling drained and discouraged. It relates to her work, and if she chooses, she doesn't have to deal with this particular circumstance again. She asks, "But isn't suffering just part of the Christian life? Don't I just have to put up with this?"

My friend is lovely and kind, smart and devoted to helping others. Her question comes from the best of intentions, and I love her for it. I've heard similar questions from people in my past work as a counselor and life coach. I've asked this kind of question myself. But this morning I have an aha moment along with my almond milk latte.

I think of a phrase about Jesus from Hebrews 12:2: "For the joy set before him he endured the cross" (NIV). Stanford psychologist Kelly McGonigal discovered people are better able to deal with stress when they're pursuing a goal.[1] We can endure the discomfort and pain of now when we think of future benefits—*the joy set before us*. When we find ourselves experiencing stress, we can pause and ask ourselves these two questions:

- *What is the joy set before me?* When I run, it's uncomfortable, but I know it will make me stronger. If someone chooses to overcome an addiction, it's challenging, but there's freedom at the finish line. If we take on a project at work because we believe in the good it can do, we're driven to make the sacrifices needed to turn it into a reality. If we envision the people our children will one day become, the dirty diapers and sleepless nights can be meaningful, not just mundane. *Being clear about the joy set before us is empowering.*
- *If I can't think of any joy set before me and this stress is optional, do I need to eliminate it from my life?* This is a somewhat scandalous question that actually applies to the conversation I had with my friend at the coffee shop, and to many other situations.

Author and researcher Marcus Buckingham did a study with thousands of women to discover what made them thrive. The results weren't what we might expect. What mattered wasn't a woman's income, marital status, whether or not she had children, or any other external factor. The women who thrived spent more time each day in moments that made them feel stronger, that led them toward more joy in the long term.

Buckingham says in *Find Your Strongest Life*, "You must face up to the fact that some moments have negative energy for you. They are emotionally draining. Trying to put a positive charge on these weak moments is, at best, a short-term survival strategy: it may help you get through the day, but, over time, it will hollow out your life."[2]

Yes, we will all experience stress and face challenges. But as women, we often do things out of guilt, obligation, a desire to please people, fear, or a false belief we have to be perfect. We put ourselves at higher risk for burnout, depression, and anxiety.

It's okay to pause and look at what's draining or discouraging us. It's necessary to let go of what continually diminishes our souls. It's wisdom, not weakness, to be intentional with our experiences, emotions, and energy. It's responsible to release what God never intended us to carry so we can move forward in love and freedom. Sometimes the most spiritual response to stress is persevering and sometimes it's walking away.

Let's dare to start asking, "What's the joy set before you? What's the joy set before me?" Then let's take the next brave step God has for us without guilt, shame, or apology.

God, show me how to look for the joy set before me so that it will help me persevere through what I'm facing now. If what I'm moving toward isn't your will or your way for me, help me know that too and turn in a new direction. Amen.

Think of a stressful situation in your life right now. What joy can you see on the other side of it?

_____

_____

_____

LET'S WALK HAND IN HAND WITH GOD toward the destination He has set before us.

KELLY BALARIE

50

stand firm

For shoes, put on the peace that comes from the Good News so that you will be fully prepared.

Ephesians 6:15

My mom and dad recently moved out of the house where I grew up. In the process, they decided the time had come for me to take the last of my childhood belongings off their hands. They showed up with a gray plastic box, and when I lifted the lid, all the memories came back. *Oh, yes, the Barbies.*

I'm a child of the eighties and had all the Barbie paraphernalia to prove it. Dresses. Apartment. Horse. Pool. Hot-pink convertible. Clearly, Barbie had a glamorous life. She also had shoes that seemed to ensure she would never enjoy a moment of it—high heels so steep they could have been tiny ski slopes. "Barbie," I said as I unpacked the box, "you need some slippers and yoga pants."

I remember loving those shoes as a little girl, dreaming of growing up to be the kind of woman who would wear them. I'm older and wiser now. I've learned to prefer shoes that actually let me stand in them without wobbling like a seasick monkey.

If an ancient Roman solder had seen those Barbie shoes, he would have been entirely confused. The shoes he would have worn, the kind the apostle Paul was likely describing when he was talking about putting on the armor of God, were entirely different. Soldiers wore leather sandals that had something like small spikes attached to the soles. More similar to soccer cleats, these shoes allowed the soldiers to hold their ground when the enemy attacked. Paul said, "For shoes, put on the peace that comes from the Good News so that you will be fully prepared" (Eph. 6:15).

What I've learned is that the shoe needs to fit not only the foot but also the occasion. Roman soldiers needed shoes for battle. Apparently, we do too. It seems ironic that *peace* is the word used to describe these shoes. I don't associate peace with a battlefield. But, really, isn't that when we need peace most? This isn't a timid peace. It's not weak. It doesn't drive a pink convertible.

No, this peace is fierce and mighty, unmovable and unstoppable. It "comes from the Good News." It's the peace that reminds us God is on our side and we will be victorious no matter what. Peace is not simply an emotion. Instead, peace is a position we take of standing on who God is, what he has promised, and who he tells us we are, no matter what happens.

How do we put on the shoes of peace? By standing firm on what's true regardless of how we feel or what's happening around us. Yes, even when it feels like we are in the middle of an all-out war. The enemy of our hearts knows he can't defeat us. His only hope is convincing us to retreat. Instead, we can dig in and refuse to move. We can stay steady and never give an inch. We can remember, "The LORD will fight for you; you need only to be still" (Exod. 14:14 NIV).

Barbie had a lot of places to go back in my childhood—like the beach (bathtub), safaris (backyard), and, of course, parties (meetups with my little brother's G.I. Joe characters). But she never went to battle. My friends and I never chose to make her a warrior. Maybe we already knew deep in our girl selves that we didn't need pretend warriors when we were destined to be real ones, already growing brave and strong.

God, you are the One who enables me to stand firm and be brave. It seems like a paradox that peace is what I need for battle, but it's true. No matter what's going on around me, keep me steady and grounded in you. Amen.

What's a truth you can stand firm on today (example: God loves me, he has a plan for my life, or he has promised me victory)?

_____

_____

_____

_____

BE KIND, for everyone you meet is fighting a hard battle.

IAN MACLAREN

51

truer stories

Think sensibly, as God has distributed a measure of faith to each one.

Romans 12:3 CSB

God brought our daughter, Lovelle, into our lives when she was twenty years old, which means I got to be a grandma much sooner than I had planned. When my granddaughter was just learning to string together stories, she told me, "Nana, I pick stawbewwies" (still working on the *r*'s). "And I saw scawy pigs." Thinking perhaps I heard wrong, I asked for clarification. "Scary pigs?" She nodded solemnly, eyes wide at the memory.

The next weekend I visited the strawberry patch myself and, sure enough, in the field next door were a few pigs—pink tails, covered in mud, snoring loudly. Not exactly a threat.

We all know kids' perceptions don't always reflect reality. But we forget the same is true for us as adults. I had my version of "scary pigs" just this morning. I'm navigating a stressful situation and told myself, "I'm going to fail. Everyone is annoyed with me. I have no idea what I'm doing."

I went for a walk so I could process my emotions. At first, I tried going to the opposite extreme by saying, "Everything is great! I'm going to do this perfectly! Everyone will cheer." But those words felt fake and hollow. Now what? I didn't want to tell myself the worst story. I didn't want to tell myself the best story. Then a question came to my heart: *What is the most beneficial story?*

I thought of Paul's words to "think sensibly, as God has distributed a measure of faith to each one" (Rom. 12:3 CSB). I'd not been, um, *thinking sensibly*. I felt like a failure, so it must be true. I felt like everyone was annoyed with me, so it must be true. I felt like I had no idea what I was doing, *so it must be true*. Have you ever done the same?

One of the perks of being a grown-up is that we are capable of telling ourselves that what we feel isn't always real. I paused and asked God, "Please help me find a different version of this story." Then I told myself, "I'm responsible for obedience, not outcomes. I can't know or control the thoughts or reactions of others. I'll do my best and then deal with whatever comes next. God is in control, and I am in charge of my choices. My work doesn't determine my worth, and I'll be loved no matter what happens." Whew.

We've all experienced stress from far more than scary pigs. We can dwell on all that has gone wrong. We can pretend everything is fine. Or we can pause and ask God to help us find a different version of our story.

Here's the secret: As humans, we naturally create fiction. God is the only One who can help us live in truth. He is still writing history. He is still writing your story too. He alone holds the pen that gets to write, "The End."

God, you are the way, the truth, and the life. When my thoughts and emotions don't align with what's true, show me a different version of the story—one that leads to hope and moving forward in faith. I trust your words and your work. Amen.

What's a story you've been telling yourself that is causing you stress? What's a different version?

_____

_____

_____

YOUR CIRCUMSTANCES MAY NOT BE THE STUFF that dreams are made of, but your life has the substance of a true love story.

LUCRETIA BERRY

52

no labels

We are citizens of heaven, where the Lord Jesus Christ lives. And we are eagerly waiting for him to return as our Savior.

Philippians 3:20

Stressed.

Depressed.

Anxious.

Frustrated.

Broken.

The labels stick to our hearts, covering our identities until we can't see who we are anymore. We come to believe that our struggles and circumstances define us. But those are just descriptions, not determinations. Who you are doesn't change based on the kind of day, week, or year you have. You are a child of God, someone loved beyond all you can imagine. *No matter what.*

A friend going through a difficult time called me. As we talked, she kept repeating the same phrase: "I guess I'm just the girl who has this struggle." I finally stopped her and said as gently as I could, "That's *where* you're at right now. It's not *who* you are."

You see, life's obstacles are temporary. Who you are is eternal.

My husband and I recently visited Canada for a few days. Imagine if we had stepped into a coffee shop and the baristas had asked, "Who are you?" and I had answered, "I'm a Canadian, y'all." They would have taken one look at my touristy tennis shoes and listened to my Southern accent, then shook their heads in bemused disagreement. I imagine you would do the same. Because you understand this: there's a difference between a visitor and a citizen. And "we are citizens of heaven," declares the apostle Paul (Phil. 3:20).

When we look at what's happening in our lives and say, "This is who I am," it's much like me declaring myself a Canadian just because I crossed the border. As my friend and fellow writer Jennifer Dukes Lee once wrote me in an email, "We don't have to be a 'citizen' of the 'place' we're standing in right now. I'm not a citizen of Sad City, a resident of Rejectionville, or a townsperson of Trouble Town. I have a citizenship in heaven."[1] Your circumstances may change, but who you truly are remains forever the same. Your identity is eternally secure in Christ.

What words have you been using to describe who you are based on where you are in life right now? Whatever comes to mind is where you're at, not who you are. It's your current location. To help shift your perspective, rewrite those words as phrases that show they aren't part of your identity. For example,

"I'm going through a stressful time right now" or "I have experienced a divorce" or "I'm battling an illness."

Once you know who you're not, it's time to ask God one of the most important questions of all: "Who am I?" Perhaps there's no more important time for seeking these answers than when we're in the middle of a bad day or a hard season. We lean into God's heart and ask, "Who am I *in spite of this*? Tell me what's true about me no matter what happens."

I love how Hebrews reassures us that "it is impossible for God to lie" (6:18). Your circumstances will lie to you. Your emotions will lie to you. Even other people will lie to you. But not God. "This hope is a strong and trustworthy anchor for our souls" (v. 19). Your identity is secure. Nothing going on in your life can change it.

God, nothing that happens to me in this life can change who you say I am. My identity is secure in you forever. On the days when I'm tempted to believe where I am is who I am, remind me of what is true. Amen.

What labels have you been putting on yourself? What does God say instead?

_____

_____

THE MORE I LEARNED ABOUT HIM, his love and unchanging character, the more I discovered my own identity.

ABBY MCDONALD

53

you have a purpose

Many are the plans in a person's heart,
but it is the LORD's purpose that prevails.
Proverbs 19:21 NIV

Stress makes us shortsighted. Our bodies are wired in such a way that when our fight-or-flight system is triggered, we react. We're not thinking noble thoughts about the meaning of life or world peace. We're just trying to save ourselves. That works well in temporary situations. The trouble is, many of us live in *chronic stress*. That means the stress reaction becomes a lifestyle, which carries a high cost. It takes a toll on our health as well as our relationships. And it makes us forget that we are on this earth for a purpose. We're here not merely to survive but to accomplish what no one else can.

Before we ever came into being, God had a purpose in mind for us. As he alone watched our bodies being formed in our mothers' wombs, he already knew what was ahead. "We are

God's handiwork, created in Christ Jesus to do good works, which God prepared in advance for us to do" (Eph. 2:10 NIV).

When life comes along and slaps us silly, it can feel as if God's purpose for us has now been canceled. But nothing can stop his purposes for us. Scripture is full of stories in which people found themselves in difficult circumstances that turned out to be part of God's mysterious plan.

Joseph's brothers sold him into slavery because of their jealousy. Then his master's wife falsely accused him, so he landed in prison. But God acted on his behalf, and he ended up second in command of the whole country, which enabled him to save the lives of God's people during a famine.

Esther got drafted into the royal harem, along with hundreds of other women. Taken away from everything she knew, she had one shot to win the king's favor. She did so and became the next queen, which eventually gave her the opportunity to rescue the Jewish people from a wicked man's plot.

Jesus himself faced death on a cross and what seemed like the ultimate defeat. Instead of being welcomed as Savior, he experienced betrayal, mistreatment, and abandonment. Yet three days later, he victoriously and joyfully rose again to rescue us all from death.

Just because your circumstances are hard doesn't mean God's purpose for you has changed. Joseph, Esther, and even Jesus could have said, "I must have done something wrong. Look at what's happening to me! I'm going to give up and just hang on until heaven." Instead, each one looked past the present and held on to an eternal perspective.

You have not been sidelined.

You have not been disqualified.

You have not been placed on the bench to wait out the rest of the game.

God's purpose for you *will* prevail. In all of history, no person has ever been able to thwart God's ultimate plan. He isn't shocked by the brokenness of this world or even by your personal failures. He can redeem and reroute as much as is needed to get you to the destination he has in mind.

That's the secret: you don't have to carry the load of living with purpose. You can embrace it, celebrate it, cling to it—but you don't have to make it happen. God is going to use you in unexpected, powerful ways.

You have a purpose.

God, sometimes life is messy, and I don't understand what's happening or how it will all work out. But I'm yours. Thank you for creating me with a purpose. Thank you that nothing and no one can destroy that purpose. You will make sure it's fulfilled. Amen.

What's a time in your life when you've seen God work out his purpose and plan for you?

_____

_____

_____

_____

I DON'T HAVE TO HAVE IT ALL TOGETHER. And I can guarantee that I have a lot of growing and refining to do. But knowing that God has called me to a specific purpose, and knowing that He will equip me along the way is enough for me right now.

KRISTIN A. SMITH

54

strength in weakness

My strength is made perfect in weakness.
2 Corinthians 12:9 NKJV

An old commercial shows a woman approaching a display of the Crown Jewels in a museum. She asks the museum worker to tell her how much they cost because she'd like to buy them. He insists, "They're not for sale, ma'am," to which she replies, "I'm not trying to haggle with you. Just shoot me a number."[1] What she doesn't understand is that the Crown Jewels are price-less because they are irreplaceable. They're not mass-produced. They're one of a kind. So are you.

As I write this, over seven billion people inhabit our planet. But there is only one you. And for as long as the world contin-ues to exist, that will remain true. God doesn't have a plan B for your life. He doesn't have a backup plan for the gifts he's placed within you. You're our one-shot wonder at getting you.

When we're stressed or going through a difficult time, we can quickly lose sight of our worth. We feel small, unseen, incapable, and of little value. It seems everyone else is doing better, has more, or is really making a difference. But not us. We withdraw and start believing we don't have anything to contribute—at least not until things are better in our lives.

But there is only one answer to the question, "When and where does God want to use me?" and it's always, "Right now, right here."

You may think you have nothing to offer. You may want to run and hide. You may tell yourself, "I'll only be in the way." But still God asks, quietly and persistently, "Will you let me use you, right here and right now?"

Your weaknesses and struggles are not reasons for him to give up on you. Instead, they're opportunities for you to show his strength in ways you simply can't on your best days. The apostle Paul wrestled with "a thorn" in his flesh (see 2 Cor. 12:7). We don't know what it was exactly, only that it was an ongoing source of difficulty for him. He begged God to take it away, and many of us are familiar with the divine response. God said, "My strength is made perfect in weakness" (2 Cor. 12:9 NKJV).

In other words, the very places and times when you feel God can use you least are when he may actually shine through you most.

When God uses us in those moments, it's humbling because we realize *it never really has been about us.* Hopefully that leads to a new sense of freedom. We can stop our striving. We can give up working so crazy hard to change the world. We can release our plans and instead open our hands to God.

We are made in the image of the God who created the universe, and there is a part of who he is that only gets shown through who we are. Sometimes that happens through our strengths. But sometimes it's through our cracks that his light shines the brightest.

God, sometimes I don't feel like I have much to give. But you are in me during those times just as you are in the moments when I feel the strongest and most capable. I want the world to receive what you have designed me to share. I yield myself to you. Use all I have to make much of you. Amen.

How have you seen God's strength in your weaknesses?

_____

_____

_____

WE ARE FRAGILE BY DESIGN! This is a huge relief, because it's consistent with my reality. I am weak, cracked, broken, and sorely lacking in any inherent strength. But it's right in the middle of that humble reality that I am most fit to reveal God's glory.

KIM HYLAND

55

a life of love

So now I am giving you a new commandment: Love each other.
Just as I have loved you, you should love each other.

John 13:34

Years ago, my grandpa celebrated his ninetieth birthday with a party. I had the privilege of being there and serving punch. That put me in a position to do a lot of listening. Over fifty people packed into his house, and each one came with a story.

"I was in your grandpa's Sunday school class forty years ago."

"I used to shop in your grandpa's bookstore, and he always encouraged me."

"I'm in the Gideons with your grandpa. We've been friends for decades!"

"I go to your grandpa's church, and he hugs me every Sunday."

"I'm your grandpa's neighbor, and he makes me laugh whenever I see him."

On and on the stories went of how my grandpa had spent his life loving well, in little and big ways. I nodded my head in agreement because I'd experienced the same. For over fifteen years, my grandpa took me out on breakfast dates to ask me how I was doing and encourage me in my faith.

My grandpa never went to Hollywood. He wasn't the CEO of a big corporation or a high-position politician. He was a regular guy in a small town who simply said yes when God asked to use him.

It turns out that doing so blessed those around him, it's also probably one of the reasons he lived so long. Research has shown that those who have strong relationships and serve others tend to live healthier, more joyful lives.

When we go through stress, it's easy to hunker down and withdraw from others. I certainly tend to respond that way. If I'm having a hard day, I'm more likely to sit on the corner of the couch with some chocolate for a private pity party than I am to reach out to those around me. I'm slowly learning that such a choice isn't beneficial.

We are made to connect with others. Daniel Goleman, author of *Social Intelligence*, says, "Our brain has been preset for kindness."[1] He goes on to share that we are always impacted by those around us. Through brain "loops," we catch each other's moods like colds. Watch two friends having an intimate conversation. Their body language almost always synchronizes without them even realizing it. What this ultimately means is that when we bring joy to others, it comes back to us in both spiritual and physical ways.

When we're stressed, we need to shift our internal state, and serving others can be one of the most effective ways to do so.

Ironically, when we need it most is often when we're least likely to do this. That can be due to lower energy (and sometimes what we really do need is simply rest). But it can also be because of a lie we believe: "I have to have it all together before I can help someone else."

Have you ever felt this way? I have. But it's simply not true. Throughout Scripture, God uses messy, broken people right in the middle of their greatest challenges. We don't need to have it all together. Wherever we are today, we can serve in some way. Even if it's just offering a smile to the nurse in our hospital room. Or making our toddler giggle when we're almost at the end of our patience. Or listening to a friend at church on Sunday morning when we'd really like to get home to our house and the couch instead.

What I've seen through my grandpa's life is that true service isn't about grand gestures; it's about a series of small choices. Most of them unseen. Many times we won't know the impact on this side of heaven. All of which add up to a lifetime of resilience and loving well.

God, I'm grateful that I don't have to go through life alone, that you created me to connect with others and share my burdens with them. Show me who I can encourage today, and help me reach out when life is stressful and I need encouragement too. Amen.

Who can you give love to today? Who do you need to receive love from?

_____

_____

_____

WE WONDER HOW TO CHANGE THE WORLD, how to
leave a mark, move the hand of God. We change the world when
we simply meet the needs of another. When we love others more
than ourselves, not expecting anything in return.

KRISTEN WELCH

56

when you're overwhelmed

*I cry to you for help
when my heart is overwhelmed.*

Psalm 61:2

Imagine a moment when you become overwhelmed. Your brain freezes. Your emotions rise. You hear an inner voice say, *This is all just too much.* We become overwhelmed when the requirements of our lives (real or perceived) feel greater than our personal resources. Feeling overwhelmed is a reality we all will face at some point. So let's talk about what's going on and what will help.

Most of us are familiar with the fight-or-flight response. But there's actually a third component to it: *freeze.* When this happens, we shut down and suddenly can't seem to think, process, or do one more thing.

Our nervous system, which is responsible for our fight-flight-freeze response, has two divisions—sympathetic and parasympathetic. When experiencing a threat, the sympathetic nervous system primes us for action and is responsible for fight and flight. If we stay in stress mode too long, the parasympathetic side of our nervous system, which is responsible for slowing us down and helping us relax, kicks in and we experience freeze.

These systems are designed to override the logical parts of our minds. That's why we can't just talk ourselves out of feeling overwhelmed with facts or force ourselves to "snap out of it." God, in all his wisdom, made us with emergency brakes that kick in automatically for our overall well-being. If we never reached the point of feeling overwhelmed, we would destroy ourselves because we would never stop.

We often become overwhelmed in the following three situations:

- *We've taken on too much.* Our to-do list is more than we can handle. Dr. Ellen Hendriksen says, "Your brain doesn't just see a to-do list; it sees a threat. It sees the threat of scarcity: not enough time, not enough energy, not enough magical ability to fit everything into twenty-four hours. Or it sees the threat of failing, the threat of disappointing others, the threat of feeling incapable."[1]

- *We've taken in too much.* Research has shown that social media and the news can contribute to the feeling of being overwhelmed. For example, one study revealed those who consumed six hours or more of media coverage about the Boston Marathon bombing had higher stress levels than those who were actually there.[2]

- *We're going too fast.* Dr. Judith Orloff says about her stressed-out patients, "When they are feeling overwhelmed one of the first aspects I address is pacing: a basic energetic rhythm I train my patients to intuitively sense. Just as heartbeat and respirations tune our physiological tempo, pacing sets our subtle energy clock's timing. Often we get caught in extremes."[3]

What helps when you're overwhelmed? First, you need to get your nervous system to stop pulling the emergency brake. To do that, it helps to focus on the present moment. As a starting place, try the following technique recommended by many mental health experts.

Pause and notice . . .

- 5 things you see (example: sky)
- 4 things you feel (example: mug)
- 3 things you hear (example: music)
- 2 things you smell (example: lotion)
- 1 thing you taste (example: coffee)

This helps our brains realize there's not an imminent threat, so they can get out of emergency mode. Then, related to the three ways we get overwhelmed, we can pause and ask ourselves these questions:

- **If we've taken *on* too much:** *What can I eliminate, delegate, or minimize today?* This can be small. For example, dinner tonight might be takeout instead of taking an hour to cook a meal.

- **If we've taken *in* too much:** *What boundaries or limitations do I need to set today?* This often means turning something off—the television, the notifications on our phone, or the light next to our bed so we can go to sleep earlier.

- **If we're going too fast:** *What's one way I can slow down today?* Ironically, this may mean *adding* one more thing to our day like a walk, bath, nap, or anything else that has a different pace.

Try different things as you answer these questions. Over time, you'll discover what works best for you. Having times when you become overwhelmed is part of being human, but you can learn to manage them. And you don't have to do it alone. As the psalmist writes,

> I cry to you for help
> when my heart is overwhelmed. (Ps. 61:2)

Pause today and recognize that being overwhelmed doesn't mean you're weak. It means you have given absolutely everything you've got. Now it's time to give yourself what you need too.

God, I'm so grateful that I, like the psalmist, can cry out to you when I'm overwhelmed. Give me the discernment to know my limits and the courage to honor them, trusting when I do so it's not weakness but wisdom. Amen.

What are your answers to the questions in today's reading?

_____

_____

_____

OFTEN, ANXIETY GETS A HOLD ON ME when I think I can handle everything on my own and then realize that I cannot. Knowing that God is with me always quiets my soul.

ANGELA NAZWORTH

57

a new way to set goals

Do not despise these small beginnings, for the LORD rejoices to see the work begin.

Zechariah 4:10

True confession: I've never been a fan of goals. When I worked in the corporate world, I remember sitting in an enthusiastic quarterly meeting. Someone put a slide on a screen with a list of numbers and percentages. At break time, a coworker walked up to me and pointed a finger in my face, grinning. "I saw you shake your head when that manager said, 'What we measure gets better!'" Oops.

What finally got me to start setting goals was realizing my default goal is 100 percent. If I don't set any goals at all, then my goal is always perfection. If you're wired the same way, you may actually need goals to put *less* pressure on yourself. What if we can do goals differently? What if they could help us *not* be so hard on ourselves?

My change in heart regarding goals also came from working with coaching clients. They would tell me of some idealistic goal they had like "I want to run a marathon in three weeks!" I would say, "I think the desire to be more active is great! Now what's the *minimum* that will make you feel like you're making progress?" The response would be something like "I could take a walk three evenings a week."

Here's the magic of identifying a minimum: it starts to build momentum. Imagine I had two clients, one who insisted on the three-week marathon goal and the other who started with the minimum. If someone asked me to bet (don't worry, I don't bet) on which one would *actually* run a marathon one day, I'd choose the walker every single time.

For myself and my clients, I've started looking at goals differently. We come up with not one goal but three: a minimum, medium, and maximum. For example, walking three nights a week is a minimum, adding one day of running is medium, and running four days a week is maximum.

When we set goals, we often act as if they're going to happen in isolation from the rest of our lives. We think of what we could do if we had no other challenges or responsibilities. But that's not how it works. When we set goals, we need to consider one additional factor—our current level of life stressors. Then *we match our goal level with our life-stressor level.*

For example, if we're in a season where we have extra free time and fewer responsibilities than usual, then we have minimum stress and could go for the maximum goal level. If our schedule is full and our responsibilities heightened, then that's maximum stress and pairs best with a minimum goal level.

Traditional systems of goal setting can feel rigid. And we all know life is not rigid. It requires us to continually adapt, shift, change, grow, slow down, speed up, juggle, try again. So if we're going to set goals, we need a method and perspective that work the same way.

"Do not despise these small beginnings, for the LORD rejoices to see the work begin" (Zech. 4:10). God's goal for our lives isn't perfection; it's growth and connection. Every effort counts. Every step matters. Every little bit of progress can be reason for rejoicing.

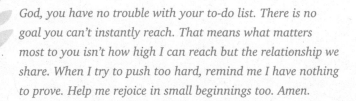

God, you have no trouble with your to-do list. There is no goal you can't instantly reach. That means what matters most to you isn't how high I can reach but the relationship we share. When I try to push too hard, remind me I have nothing to prove. Help me rejoice in small beginnings too. Amen.

Think of a goal in your life. Try adjusting it using the minimum, medium, maximum method, and consider your level of life stressors as you do.

PERFECTION WAS NEVER A WORTHWHILE GOAL. Let's provide room for mistakes and growing through them. Let's choose which things matter and not worry about what others may think. Let's give each other a little grace and while we're at it, let's pour some over our own heart too.

SUZANNE ELLER

58

letting go of expectations

Be silent before the LORD and wait expectantly for him.

Psalm 37:7 CSB

Before the COVID-19 pandemic, we didn't think twice about walking into a store or party with friends. We knew the term *social media* but not *social distancing*. Masks were still for surgeons and bank robbers. We made resolutions and set goals. We imagined what the future would hold—and we were wrong.

We all live with an internal set of expectations, which psychologists describe as strong beliefs in particular outcomes. I know this, in part, because in my early twenties, I went to counseling for the first time. I was struggling with anxiety and depression. I don't remember everything my counselor said, but one vivid image remains in my mind.

My counselor pulled out a yellow notepad and drew a horizontal line across it. Then she drew a series of vertical lines reaching toward it but never quite getting there. She tapped the horizontal line and said, "These are your expectations." Then she pointed toward the vertical lines and added, "This is reality." Her point? Until I lowered my expectations, especially of myself, I would continue to battle anxiety and depression. At that time in my life, my expectation was perfection. And, as you know, real life never quite gets there either.

I recently read an article by Justin E. Smith in which he talked about the difficulties of the COVID-19 pandemic. But he also included a quote I still can't stop thinking about. He said,

> I find that there is liberation in this suspension of more or less everything. In spite of it all, we are free now. Any fashion, sensibility, ideology, set of priorities, worldview or hobby that you acquired prior to March 2020, and that may have by then started to seem to you cumbersome, dull, inauthentic, a drag: you are no longer beholden to it. You can cast it off entirely and no one will care; likely, no one will notice. Were you doing something out of mere habit, conceiving your life in a way that seemed false to you? You can stop doing that now.[1]

Yes, this season of history has been challenging in more ways than we ever could have imagined. I hope we never have another like it. But perhaps the hidden gift in it, in any time of upheaval and change, is an unexpected freedom from some expectations that weighed us down and held us back.

If that's true, what do we do now? When I look at Scripture, I find a different way of living. "Be silent before the LORD and wait expectantly for him" (Ps. 37:7 CSB). Instead of wearing myself out with expectations, I can live *expectantly*. What's the difference? Expectations are of our own making; living expectantly means opening ourselves to what God will do.

Isn't faith really the ultimate example of living expectantly? The Jewish people expectantly watched for a Messiah. Mary and Joseph expectantly waited for their son to come. The wise men expectantly followed the star.

I don't know what the world will be like when you're reading this, but I know there will still be expectations and the opportunity to live instead with expectancy. This is my simple prayer for this season and whatever one you're in today. *God, give me the courage to let go of expectations and live expectantly.* Will you pray this with me?

God, I will say it again—give me the courage to let go of expectations and live expectantly. You alone know the future. You hold the whole world, and my little life, in your hands. When I'm tempted to give in to demands you never placed on me, remind me of what is true and set me free. Amen.

What's an expectation you need to let go of that's weighing you down? What would it look like to live expectantly in that situation instead?

_____

_____

_____

WHAT I'M BURNING DOWN ARE THE EXPECTATIONS I've long held for who I had to be, what people needed me to be, and the distance those expectations created between God and me, and between the people I love and me, and between the beauty of the world and me.

SHAUNA NIEQUIST

without judgment

There is no judgment against anyone who believes in him.

John 3:18

The youth group meeting room is dark, and someone slips a tape into a VCR. The square television screen flickers to life, and the giggles from the back row cease. It's the 1980s, and our eyebrows raise in surprise as we watch a teenager stand before the judgment seat of God. Every bad thing she has ever done is projected onto a wall for everyone to see. We swallow hard and hope God hasn't read our diaries. The message is clear: the day of judgment is something to be feared.

Only for believers, it's not. I sat in another darkened room recently, the sanctuary of our church, and watched a verse projected onto a screen that tells an entirely different story about the day of judgment. "Then God will give to each one whatever praise is due" (1 Cor. 4:5). I thought perhaps someone on the church staff had made a mistake. Wasn't it supposed to be "God

231

will give to each one whatever judgment is due"? But, no, in every translation the message is clear. I even looked up every verse in the entire Bible that has the word *judgment* in it just to be sure I wasn't missing anything. Throughout Scripture, the message is the same. As believers, when we stand before God, it will be a time of affirmation, not condemnation.

Our daughter runs half marathons, and we wait for her at the finish line. Watching each runner come in always brings tears to my eyes. Because no matter how weary they are, the reaction is the same. We cheer, and then inevitably someone they love finds them, embraces them, and says something like "Well done!" I have never heard a runner criticized at the finish line.

The scene is reminiscent of the parable where a master goes away and entrusts his servants with what belongs to him. When he returns and speaks to a trustworthy servant, he is full of praise: "Well done, my good and faithful servant. You have been faithful in handling this small amount, so now I will give you many more responsibilities. Let's celebrate together!" (Matt. 25:21).

I realized my false beliefs about the judgment often stressed me out and stole my peace. It felt like the Christian life was the spiritual version of a mama saying, "Wait until your father gets home!" In other words, you're not in trouble now, but you just wait. But the scandalous beauty of the gospel is, "There is no judgment against anyone who believes in him" (John 3:18).

When we get to heaven, it will be a joyful homecoming. It will not be about the mistakes we've made but about the wonder that we made it through this life. We crossed the finish line and the great cloud of witnesses can cheer. We'll see Jesus face-to-face at last. It won't feel like going to the principal's office; it will feel like we're in the presence of the Prince of Peace—because we will be.

On the cross when he took God's wrath for us, when he died for our sins, Jesus said, "It is finished" (John 19:30). There is no eternal "PS" to that statement. There's not an "oops, I forgot that one really terrible thing you did." We are right with God today. We are right with God tomorrow. We are right with God for all eternity.

The story that will be told when we get to heaven won't be one of judgment; it will be one of victory. It won't be about everything we've done wrong; it will be about all Jesus has done for us. It won't be about guilt and what we lack; it will be about grace and love far beyond what we can even imagine.

God, thank you that because I've trusted in Jesus as my Savior, I can be absolutely at peace about standing before you one day. I so look forward to that time, and I thank you that your grace will sustain me until I get there. I'm so grateful for your love and faithfulness. Amen.

What is a time when someone cheered you on or supported you? How does it feel to imagine God doing the same for you?

THERE IS ONLY GRACE, and when grace is at the forefront, there's a light that shines in our eyes. There's a light on the path in front of we who are in Christ, so we can see things for what they really are. . . . I am forgiven.

AMBER HAINES

60

new every morning

Because of the LORD's great love we are not consumed,
   for his compassions never fail.
They are new every morning;
   great is your faithfulness.

Lamentations 3:22–23 NIV

I'm watching the sky turn orange soon after my grandson, Clement, is born. I think of his dark hair, curious eyes, the way his hands curl into little fists. I think, too, of the difficulties of his birth and how he's now safe. He feels like a tiny miracle in my arms.

I think of how Lamentations says God's mercies are new every morning. I've always thought of this in literal terms, that we wake up to another round of grace every day. I believe that's true, but I wonder if those words mean more than that as well. Whenever we make it through a stressful moment in life, isn't it a new morning?

I think of the worries I had for my grandson and how he is here now, healthy and strong.

I recall something I struggled with for years and finally beat.

I remember seasons of grief or frustration, which finally gave way to hope and light.

Aren't those all mornings full of God's mercy? Psalm 30:5 says,

> Weeping may last through the night,
>> but joy comes with the morning.

I think of the ultimate morning, the one three days after Jesus hung on a cross. A day when the disciples thought all had been lost, the darkness had won. Then came the resurrection.

We experience mourning, yes, but we are ultimately people of the morning. Even when the story ends in tragedy, it is only for this life. We have a forever morning coming.

A few years ago, Mark and I went on another trip to the beach. I'm not an early riser, but we climbed out of bed and quickly made coffee. Then we walked toward the shore, the sand still cool beneath our feet. We were joined by many others—silver-haired seniors in straw hats, parents holding the hands of their children, the occasional dog leaping into the surf. All different ages, colors, sizes, stories. What we all seemed to have in common was a draw toward the sunrise.

I think this is a picture of humanity, of how we live in this world. No matter how hard this world gets, we keep finding our way through the dark. We keep moving toward the light.

We keep believing that what looks like an ending could really be a beginning.

Research shows what we think about first thing in the morning influences the course of our day. Finding a simple routine to do as soon as we wake up, like writing down three things we're grateful for, can help. We choose to fix our eyes on the horizon of the future, look for the first light breaking through the clouds, believe in what we can't yet fully see. Oh, of course we'll still experience tears, anger, and disappointment sometimes. That's part of being human too. But we never give up hope.

A new morning is always coming. The sun will rise again, and so will we.

God, you have seen everything that has ever happened on this earth. You know how dark the night can get. Yet you bring light again every day to this world, to my life. Thank you for the gift of new starts and unending hope. No matter what comes, the morning will too. Amen.

What's a fresh start, a moment of hope, a "morning" you've experienced in your life?

LIFE CAN BE HARD and come with many questions. In the midst of the challenges I faced, I saw God at work in ways I didn't know were possible. I learned to trust him because he's faithful and in control. He never left me. One thing I know to be true is that every day I have a God who knows my situations better than I do and unrelentingly loves me through them. His mercies are new every morning.

BROOKE NICHOLLS

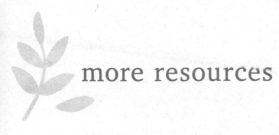

more resources

Do you want more help dealing with stress in your life?
For additional tools and resources that go with this book,
visit holleygerth.com/stress.

acknowledgments

To my editor, Jennifer Leep, thank you for a decade of doing books together. You're not only the person whose perspective makes everything I write better, but you're also a dear and trusted friend.

To my wonderful team at Revell—especially Wendy Wetzel, Amy Ballor, Eileen Hanson, Patti Brinks, and Kelli Smith—I'm so grateful for the years we've spent together, and I look forward to what's ahead.

To my virtual assistant, Kaitlyn Bouchillon, your diligence, excellence, creativity, and friendship help more than you could ever know. I appreciate all you do.

To Mom and Dad, thanks for teaching me that love is powerful and kindness is courageous, and for praying for me through every adventure.

To my grandmother, Eula Armstrong, you are an example of resilience and following Jesus for a lifetime. Thank you for all your prayers.

To my daughter, Lovelle, you're a gift, and God knew exactly what our family needed—brave, bright-shining, joy-bringing, beautiful you!

To my grandkids, Eula and Clement, I can't wait to see who God created you to be. You're already a delight.

To my husband, Mark, there are hardly enough words to describe all you are to me. Partner, friend, encourager, and the man I will be in love with all my life. I'm thankful every day to share this adventure with you.

To my local and faraway friends, thanks for being cheerleaders, advisors, and prayer warriors while I wrote this book.

To all my readers, thank you for helping shape this book through all the wisdom you offered, insights you gave, and stories you shared.

Most of all, to God, thank you for your faithful love that sees me through whatever I face. Nothing is impossible with you.

notes

Chapter 1 What You Need in Every Stressful Moment

1. Melissa Spoelstra, *The Names of God: His Character Revealed* (Nashville: Abingdon Press, 2020), 86.

Chapter 3 Helpful Responses You Can Use

1. Kelly McGonigal, *The Upside of Stress: Why Stress Is Good for You, and How to Get Good at It* (New York: Avery, 2016), 51.

2. McGonigal, *Upside*, 156.

Chapter 4 What True Peace Means

1. Tim Keller, "The Meaning of Shalom in the Bible," New International Version, accessed December 7, 2020, https://www.thenivbible.com/meaning-shalom-bible/.

2. Mark Schatzman, "Prince of Peace," sermon, Fellowship Bible Church of NWA, December 8, 2018.

Chapter 5 The Power of Your Perspective

1. Martin E. P. Seligman, Susan Nolen-Hoeksema, and Joan S. Girgus, "Learned Helplessness in Children: A Longitudinal Study of Depression, Achievement, and Explanatory Style," *Journal of Personality and Social Psychology* 51, no. 2 (1986): 435–42.

2. Christopher Peterson, Martin E. P. Seligman, and George E. Vaillant, "Pessimistic Explanatory Style Is a Risk Factor for Illness: A Thirty-Five-Year Longitudinal Study," *Journal of Personality and Social Psychology* 55, no. 1 (1988): 23–27.

3. Martin E. P. Seligman and Peter Schulman, "Explanatory Style as a Predictor of Productivity and Quitting among Life Insurance Agents," *Journal of Personality and Social Psychology* 50, no. 4 (1986): 832–38.

Chapter 6 Satisfy Your Soul Thirst

1. Susan Schoenian, "Feeding and Watering Equipment," Sheep 201: A Beginner's Guide to Raising Sheep," accessed December 7, 2020, http://www.sheep101 .info/201/feedwaterequip.html.

2. John Ortberg, *Soul Keeping: Caring for the Most Important Part of You* (Grand Rapids: Zondervan, 2014), 20.

Chapter 7 Understanding Anxiety

1. Dr. Joseph Goldberg, "How Worrying Affects the Body," WebMD, accessed December 7, 2020, https://www.webmd.com/balance/guide/how-worrying -affects-your-body#1.

2. Ana Gotter and Dr. Debra Rose Wilson, "Box Breathing," HealthLine, June 17, 2020, https://www.healthline.com/health/box-breathing#steps.

Chapter 8 Get Your Goliaths

1. Will van der Hart and Rob Waller, *The End of Worry: Why We Worry and How to Stop* (Brentwood, TN: Howard Books, 2013), 38–39.

2. Holley Gerth, *Fear, I'm Over You* (Grand Rapids: Revell, 2021), Day 4, Kindle.

Chapter 9 Optimize . . . or Not

1. Emily Lehman, "Optimize Now: The Never-Ending Pursuit of the Perfect Lifestyle," Verily, January 13, 2020, https://verilymag.com/2020/01/daily-routines -obsession-optimizing-apps-technology-burnout-culture.

Chapter 10 Making Friends with Frustration

1. Gretchen Rubin, "Podcast 270: Very Special Episode with Great Advice for Graduates," *Happier with Gretchen Rubin*, April 22, 2020, https://gretchenrubin .com/podcast-episode/270-vse-advice-for-graduates.

2. Rubin, "Podcast 270."

Chapter 12 Come, Lord

1. Suzie Eller's Facebook page, accessed November 16, 2019, https://www .facebook.com/tsuzanneeller/posts/10157387436353580.

Chapter 13 Going Dormant

1. Eileen Campbell, "How Do Trees Survive Winter?," Treehugger, updated May 10, 2020, https://www.mnn.com/earth-matters/wilderness-resources/stories/how-do-trees-survive-winter.

Chapter 18 Handling Conflict

1. Ellie Lisitsa, "The Four Horsemen: The Antidotes," The Gottman Institute, April 26, 2013, https://www.gottman.com/blog/the-four-horsemen-the-antidotes/.
2. Holley Gerth, *Fiercehearted: Live Fully, Love Bravely* (Grand Rapids: Revell, 2017), 20–21.

Chapter 23 You Don't Have to Work So Hard

1. Zach Brittle, "Turn Towards Instead of Away," The Gottman Institute, April 1, 2015, https://www.gottman.com/blog/turn-toward-instead-of-away/.

Chapter 24 Overcoming Negativity

1. Margie Warrell, "Is Negativity Bias Sabotaging Your Success?," *Forbes*, September 30, 2017, https://www.forbes.com/sites/margiewarrell/2017/09/30/combat-negativity-bias/#2974e90234a8.
2. Hara Estroff Marano, "Our Brain's Negativity Bias," *Psychology Today*, June 9, 2016, https://www.psychologytoday.com/us/articles/200306/our-brains-negative-bias.

Chapter 27 God Will Lift You Up

1. *Lexico*, s.v. "consolation," accessed February 1, 2021, https://www.lexico.com/definition/consolation.

Chapter 28 Out of Order

1. Gretchen Rubin, *Better Than Before: What I Learned about Making and Breaking Habits—To Sleep More, Quit Sugar, Procrastinate Less, and Generally Build a Happier Life* (New York: Broadway Books, 2015), 66.

Chapter 31 Helpful Boundaries

1. Henry Cloud and John Townsend, *Boundaries: When to Say Yes, How to Say No* (Grand Rapids: Zondervan, 2017), 31.

Chapter 36 Selah for Your Soul

1. Jason Soroski, "What Does Selah Mean in the Bible and Why Is It Important?," Crosswalk.com, October 10, 2018, https://www.crosswalk.com/faith/bible-study/what-does-selah-mean.html.

Chapter 38 Just Be Faithful

1. Eugene Peterson, *A Long Obedience in the Same Direction: Discipleship in an Instant Society* (Downers Grove, IL: InterVarsity, 2019), chap. 1, Kindle.

Chapter 40 A New Perspective

1. Linda Bloom and Charlie Bloom, "Reframing: The Transformative Power of Suffering," *Psychology Today*, December 14, 2017, https://www.psychologytoday.com/us/blog/stronger-the-broken-places/201712/reframing.

Chapter 41 When Life Gets Hard

1. Henry Cloud and John Townsend, *How People Grow: What the Bible Reveals about Personal Growth* (Grand Rapids: Zondervan, 2001), 82.
2. Cloud and Townsend, *How People Grow*, 40–41.

Chapter 46 Anger Is Okay

1. Gary J. Oliver and H. Norman Wright, *Good Women Get Angry: A Woman's Guide to Handling Her Anger, Depression, Anxiety, and Stress* (Ann Arbor, MI: Servant Publishing, 1996), 13.
2. "Anger: A Secondary Emotion," Conflict Resolution Education, accessed December 15, 2020, http://creducation.net/resources/anger_management/anger_a_secondary_emotion.html.
3. Jennifer Watson, "Gratitude When You Have an Attitude," *More Than Small Talk* podcast, November 7, 2019, http://www.klrc.com/podcasts/more-than-small-talk.
4. Oliver and Wright, *Good Women*, 13–14.

Chapter 48 Water-Walking

1. John Ortberg, *If You Want to Walk on Water, You've Got to Get Out of the Boat* (Grand Rapids: Zondervan, 2014), 17.
2. Ortberg, *If You Want to Walk on Water*, 17.

Chapter 49 The Joy Ahead

1. Kelly McGonigal, *The Upside of Stress: Why Stress Is Good for You, and How to Get Good at It* (New York: Avery, 2016), 143.

2. Marcus Buckingham, *Find Your Strongest Life: What the Happiest and Most Successful Women Do Differently* (Nashville: Thomas Nelson, 2009), 88.

Chapter 52 No Labels

1. Jennifer Dukes Lee, email to the author, August 14, 2013. Used by permission.

Chapter 54 Strength in Weakness

1. "Crown Jewels Straight Talk Commercial," 0:02, YouTube video, posted by MrLongboard50 on October 30, 2011, http://www.youtube.com/watch?v=Hz6RRU5H37A.

Chapter 55 A Life of Love

1. Daniel Goleman, *Social Intelligence: The New Science of Human Relationships* (New York: Bantam Dell, 2006), 60.

Chapter 56 When You're Overwhelmed

1. Ellen Hendriksen, "Feeling Overwhelmed? Here Are Seven Remedies," *Scientific American*, August 5, 2017, https://www.scientificamerican.com/article/feeling-overwhelmed-here-are-7-remedies/.

2. Alison E. Holman, Dana Rose Garfin, and Roxane Cohen Silver, "Media's Role in Broadcasting Acute Stress Following the Boston Marathon Bombings," *Proceedings of the National Academy of Sciences* 111, no. 1 (2014): 93–98; Betty Pfefferbaum, Elana Newman, Summer D. Nelson, Pascal Nitiéma, Rose L. Pfefferbaum, and Ambreen Rahman, "Disaster Media Coverage and Psychological Outcomes: Descriptive Findings in the Extant Research," *Current Psychiatry Reports* 16, no. 9 (2014): 1–7.

3. Dr. Judith Orloff, "The Secret to Managing Being Overwhelmed," *Psychology Today*, October 31, 2016, https://www.psychologytoday.com/us/blog/emotional-freedom/201610/the-secret-managing-being-overwhelmed?amp=.

Chapter 58 Letting Go of Expectations

1. Justin E. Smith, "It's All Just Beginning," *The Point Magazine*, March 25, 2020, thepointmag.com/examined-life/its-all-just-beginning/.

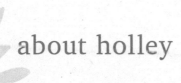

about holley

Holley Gerth loves humans, words, and good coffee. She's a *Wall Street Journal* bestselling author, life coach, and counselor with a master of science degree in mental health. Holley cofounded the groundbreaking online community (in)courage, which had almost one million page views in its first six months, and cohosts the *More Than Small Talk* podcast. Holley is also wife to Mark, mom to Lovelle, and Nana to Eula and Clement.

Connect with
HOLLEY

HolleyGerth.com

@HolleyGerth

YOU DON'T HAVE TO SETTLE FOR "I'M FINE."